FOR ORGANS, PIANOS & ELECTRONIC KEYBOARDS

E-Z PLAY® TODAY

150

THE BEST BIG BAND SONGS EVER

W9-BXM-433

This publication is not for sale in
the EC and/or Australia
or New Zealand.

ISBN 0-7935-1459-2

HAL•LEONARD®
CORPORATION
7777 W. BLUEMOUND RD. P.O. BOX 13819 MILWAUKEE, WI 53213

Visit Hal Leonard Online at
www.halleonard.com

CONTENTS

THE BEST BIG BAND SONGS EVER

Aquellos Ojos Verdes
(Green Eyes)

Music by Nilo Menendez
Spanish Words by Adolfo Utrera
English Words by E. Rivera and E. Woods

Registration 3
Rhythm: Rhumba or Latin

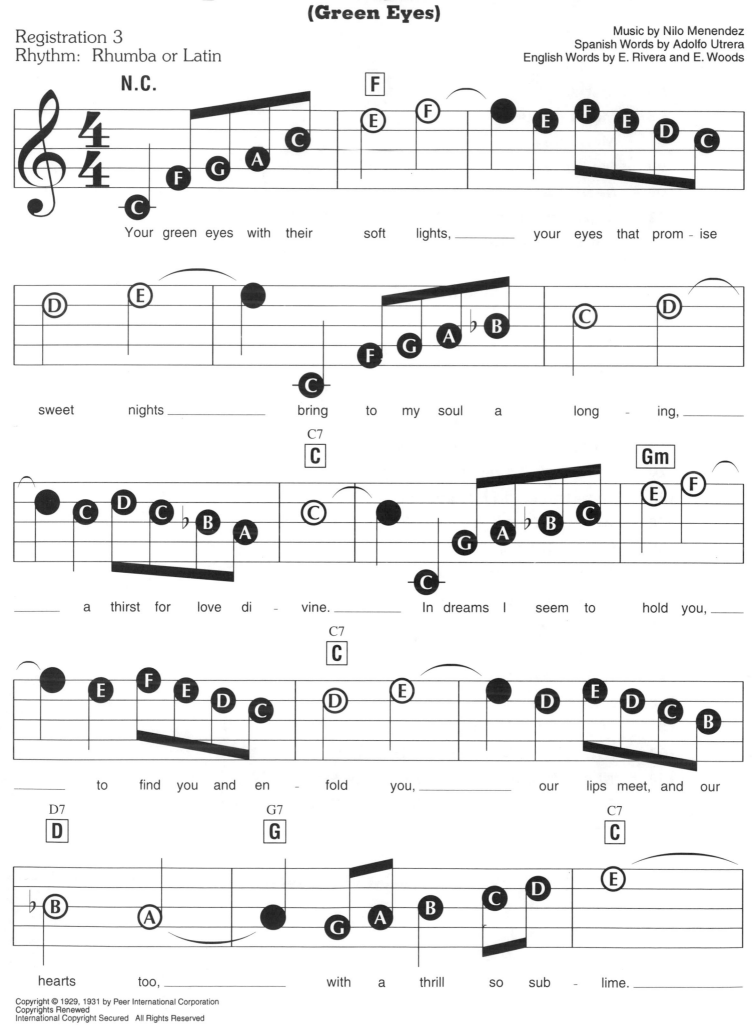

Your green eyes with their soft lights, _____ your eyes that prom - ise

sweet nights _____ bring to my soul a long - ing, _____

_____ a thirst for love di - vine. _____ In dreams I seem to hold you, _____

_____ to find you and en - fold you, _____ our lips meet, and our

hearts too, _____ with a thrill so sub - lime. _____

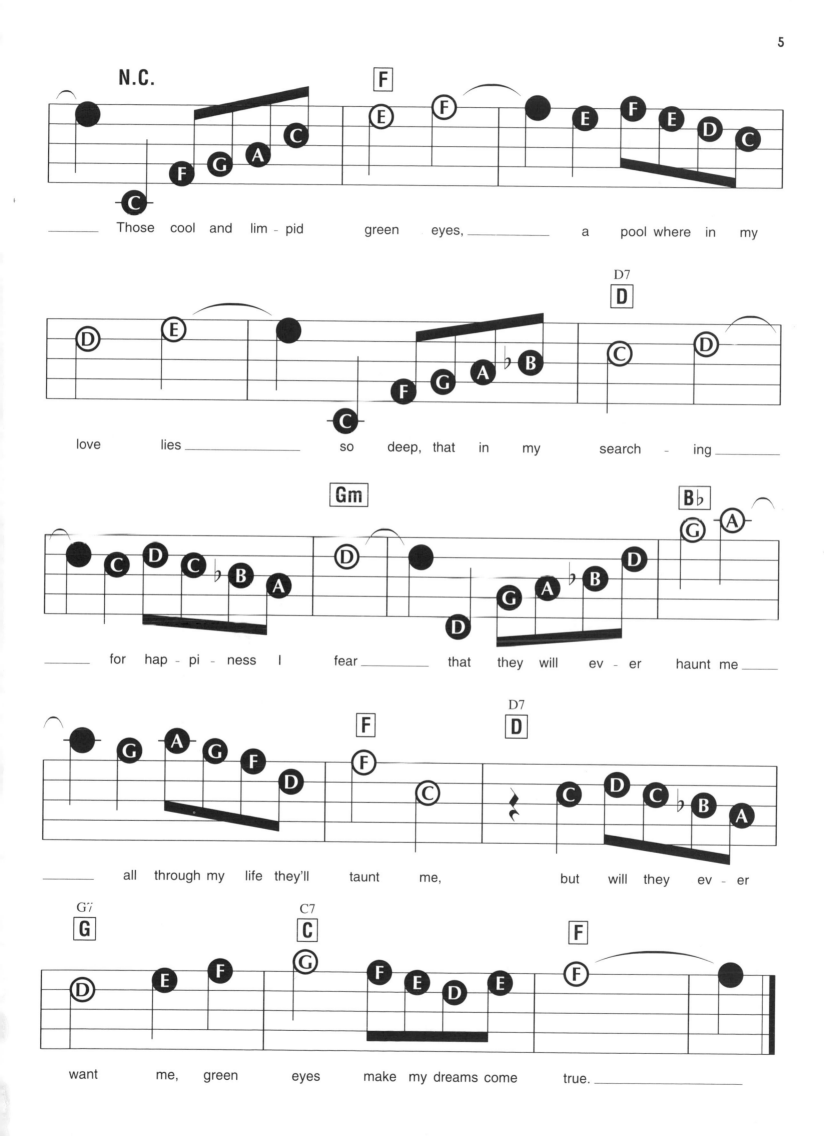

Angry

Registration 3
Rhythm: Swing or Jazz

Words by Dudley Mecum
Music by Jules Cassard, Henry Brunies and Merritt Brunies

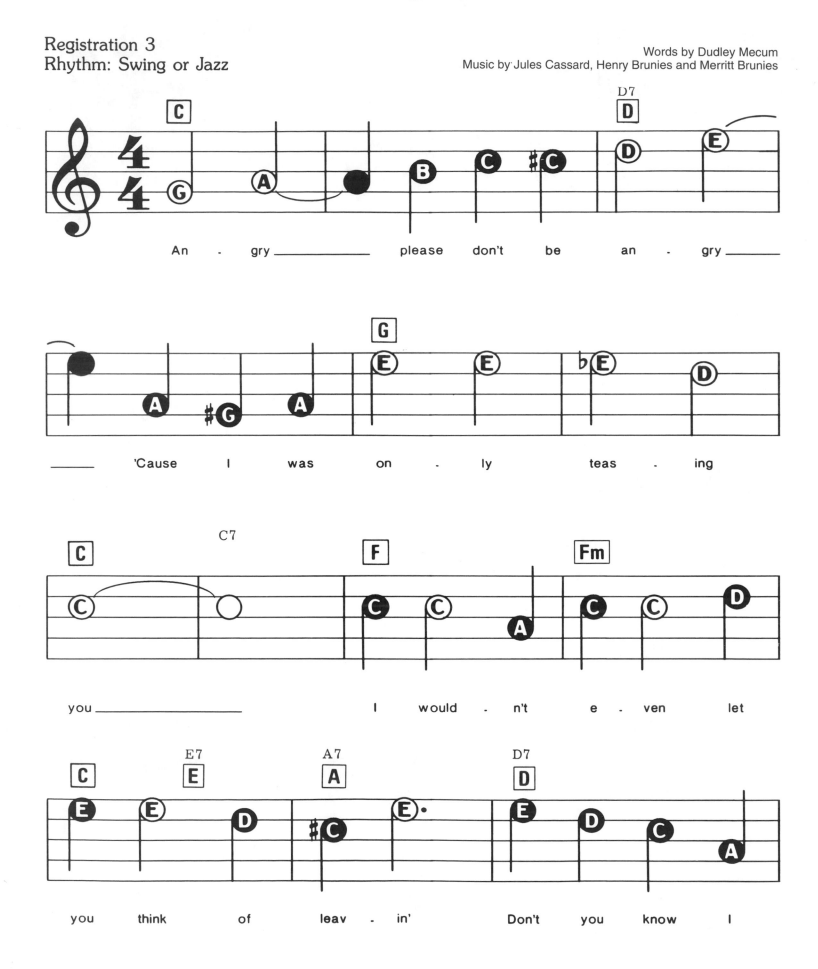

7

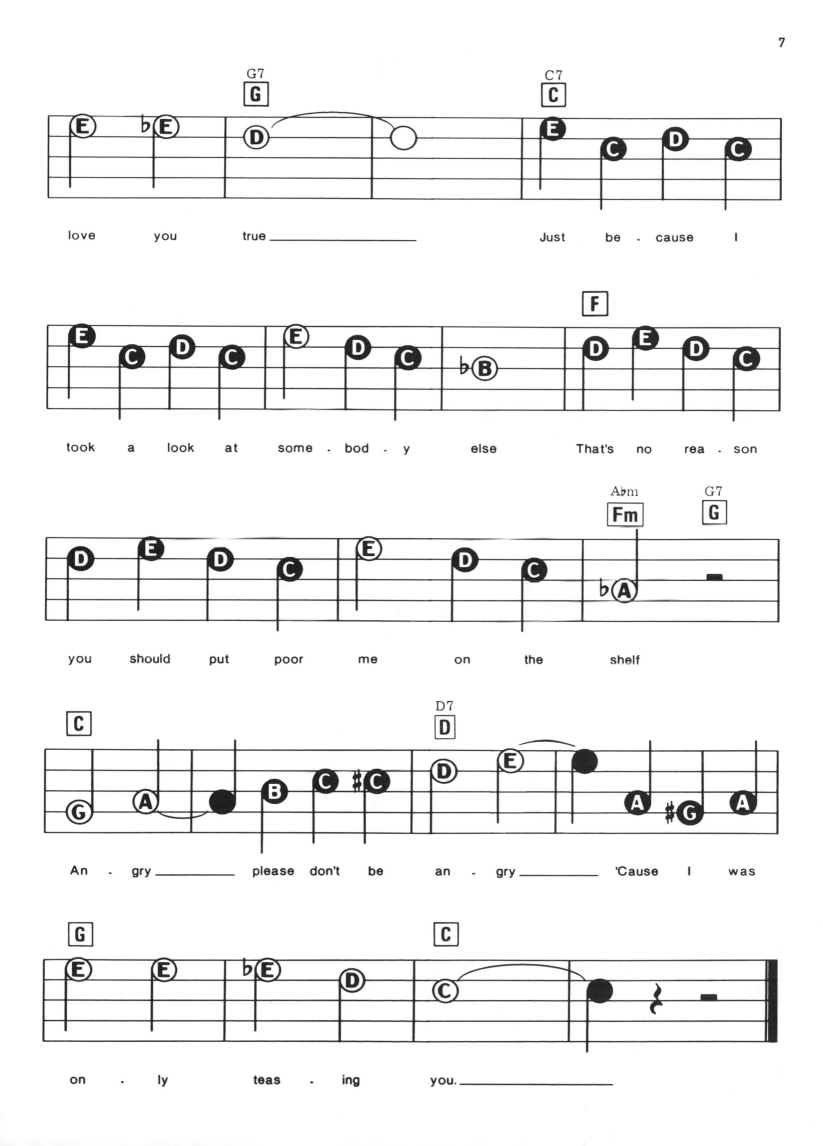

Alright, Okay, You Win

Registration 7
Rhythm: Swing

Words and Music by Sid Wyche
and Mayme Watts

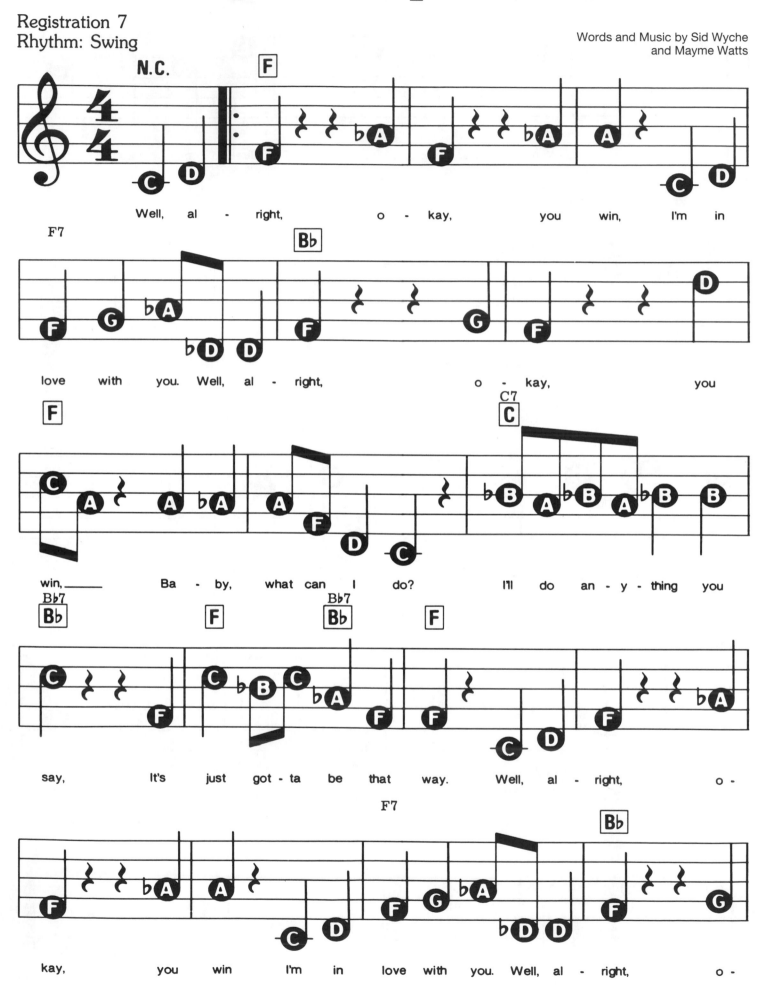

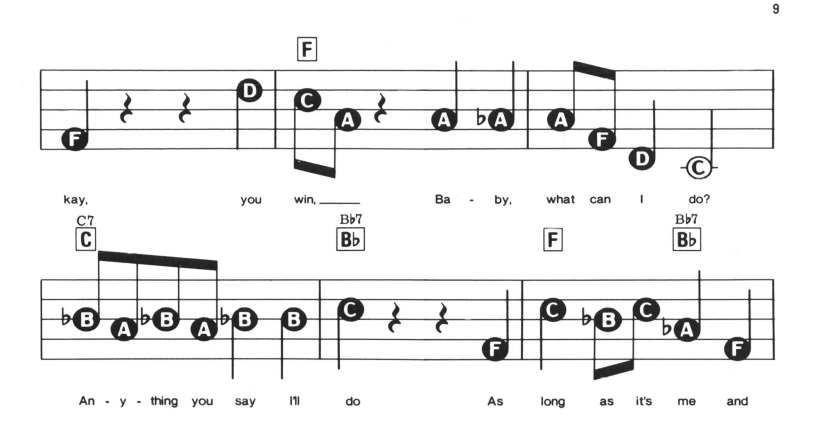

kay,   you win, _____   Ba - by, what can I do?

An - y - thing you say I'll do   As long as it's me and

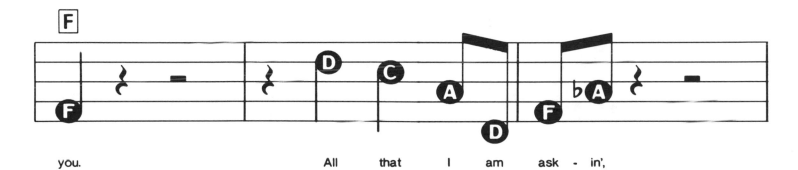

you.   All that I am ask - in',

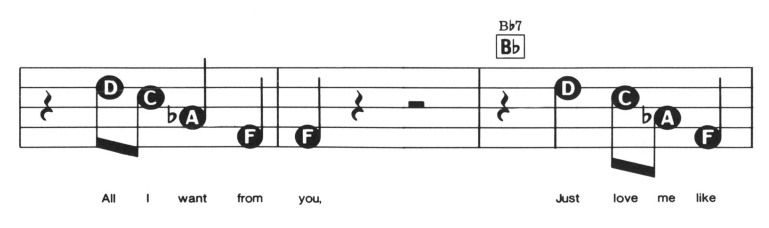

All I want from you,   Just love me like

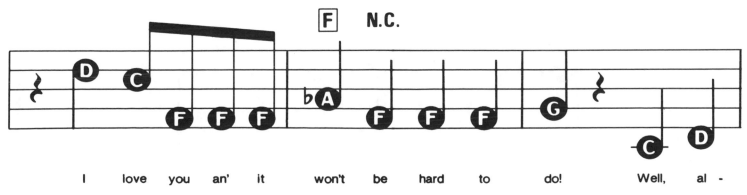

I love you an' it won't be hard to do!   Well, al -

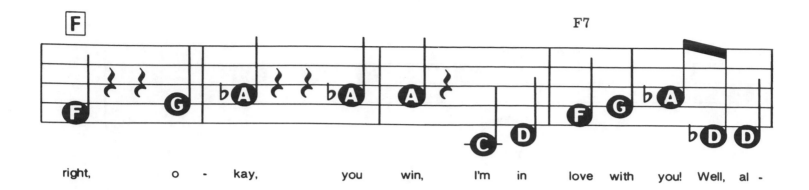

right,   o - kay,   you win,   I'm   in   love   with   you! Well, al -

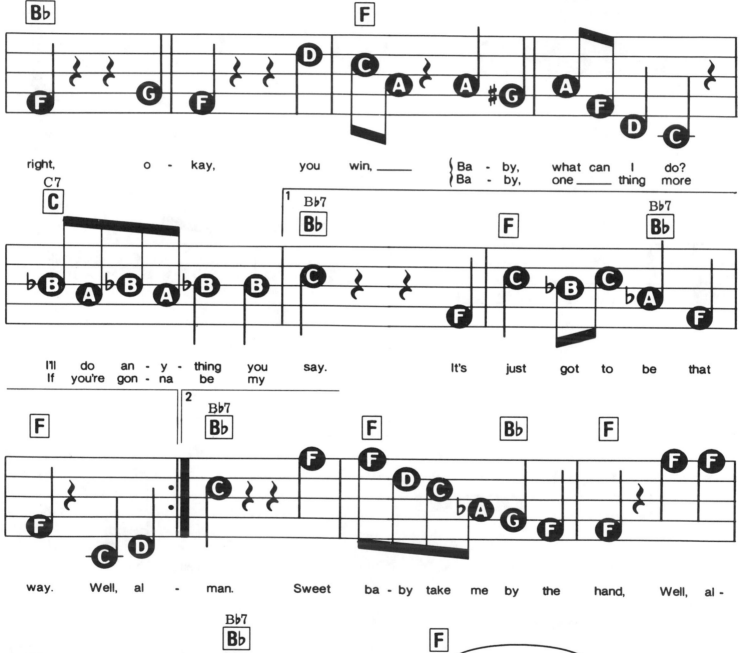

right,   o - kay,   you win, _____ { Ba - by,   what can   I   do?
                                            { Ba - by,   one ____ thing more

I'll   do   an - y - thing   you   say.   It's   just   got   to   be   that
If   you're   gon - na   be   my

way.   Well, al -   man.   Sweet   ba - by   take   me   by   the   hand,   Well, al -

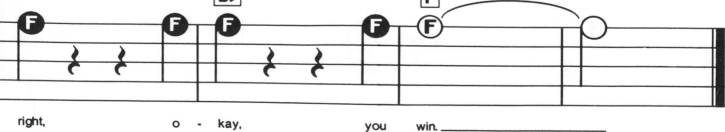

right,   o - kay,   you win. _____

Boogie Woogie Bugle Boy

Registration 7
Rhythm: Shuffle or Fox Trot

Words and Music by Don Raye
and Hughie Prince

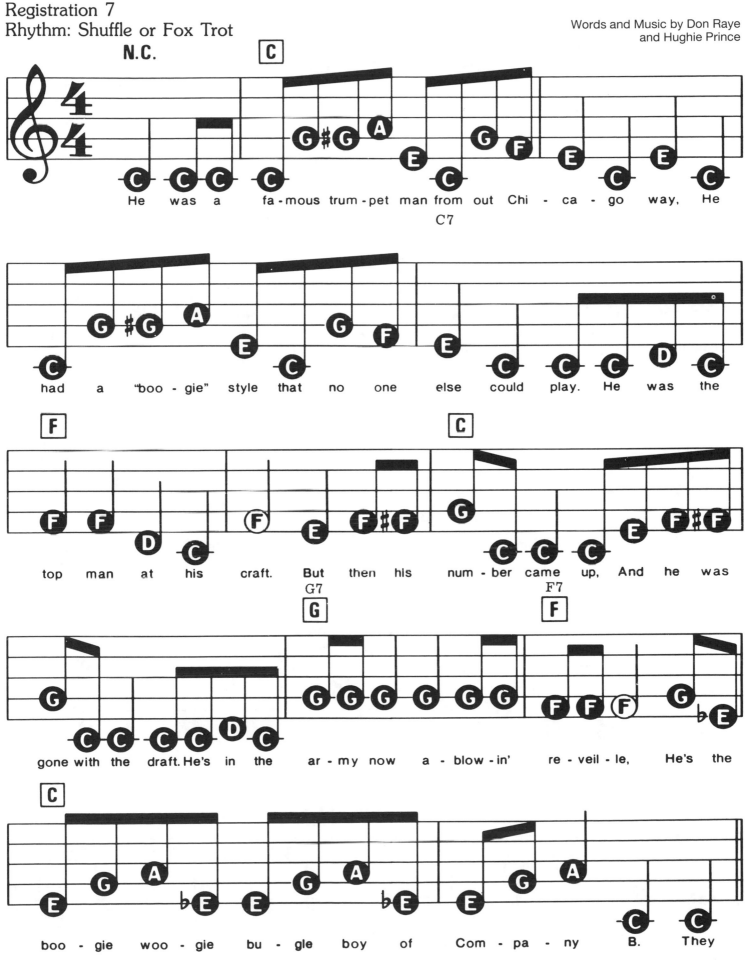

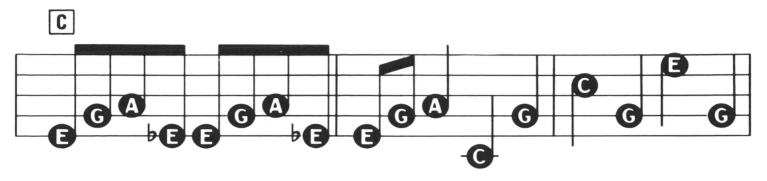

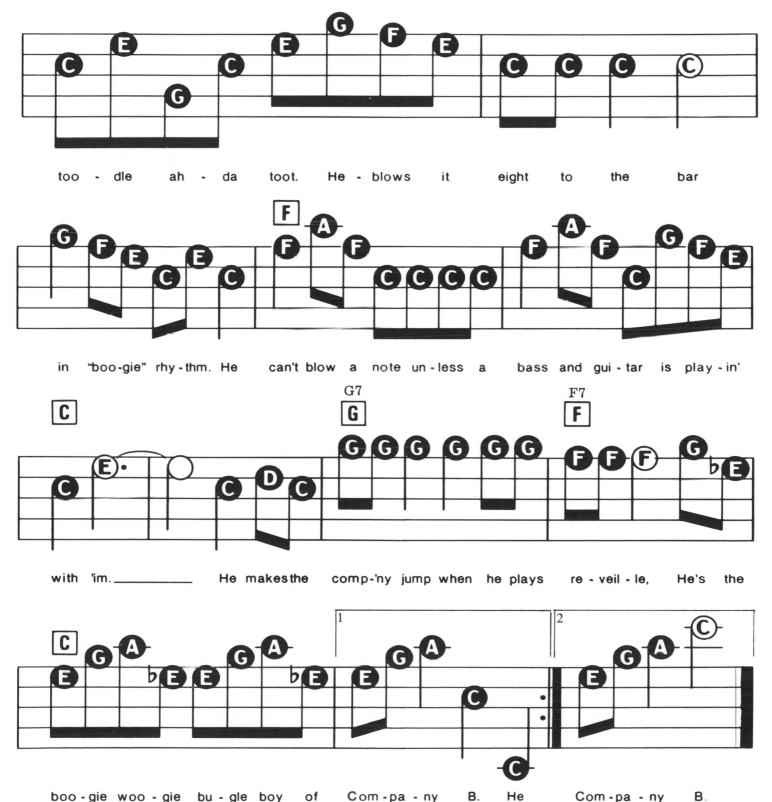

Caravan
from SOPHISTICATED LADIES

Registration 7
Rhythm: Ballad or Fox Trot

Words and Music by Duke Ellington,
Irving Mills and Juan Tizol

15

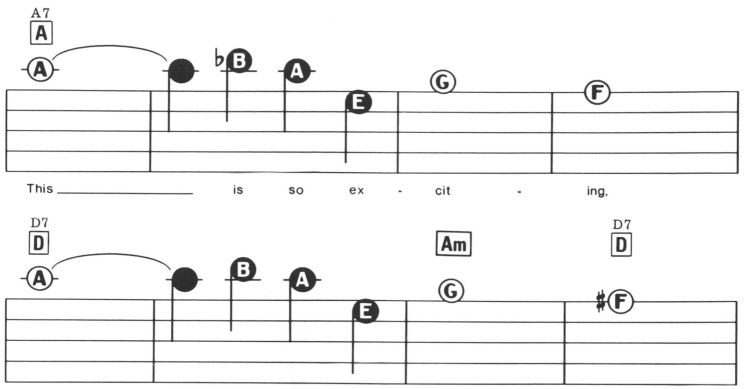

This _____ is so ex - cit - ing,

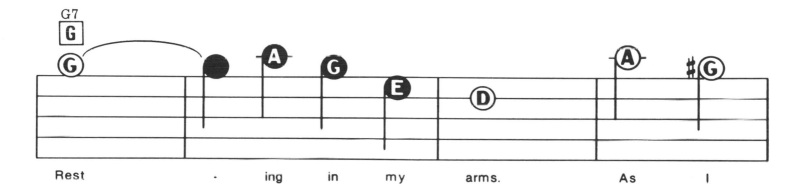

You _____ are so in - vit - ing,

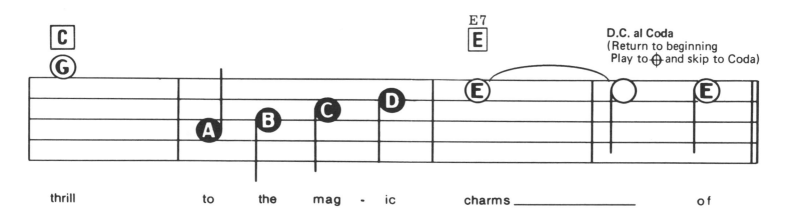

Rest - ing in my arms. As I

D.C. al Coda
(Return to beginning
 Play to ⊕ and skip to Coda)

thrill to the mag - ic charms _____ of

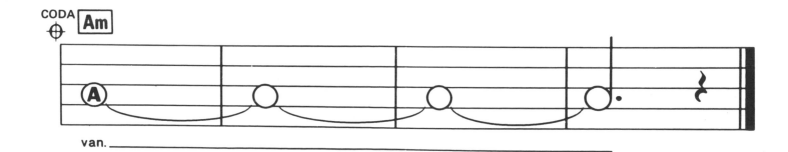

van. _____

Basin Street Blues

Registration 1
Rhythm: Swing or Fox Trot

Words and Music by
Spencer Williams

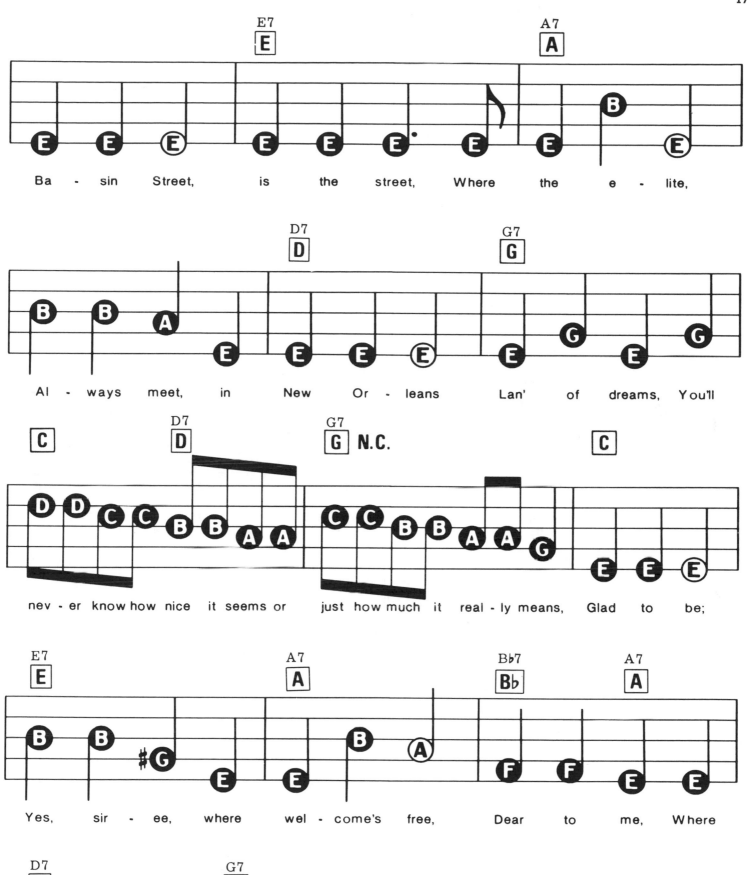

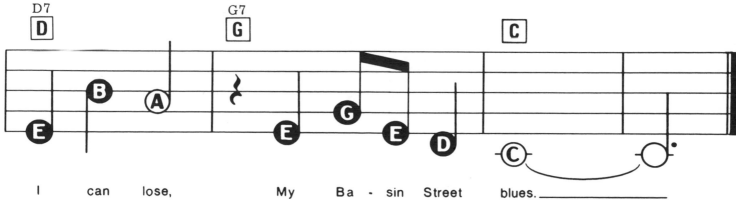

Blue Champagne

Words and Music by Grady Watts,
Frank Ryerson and Jimmy Eaton

Registration 3
Rhythm: Ballad or Slow Rock

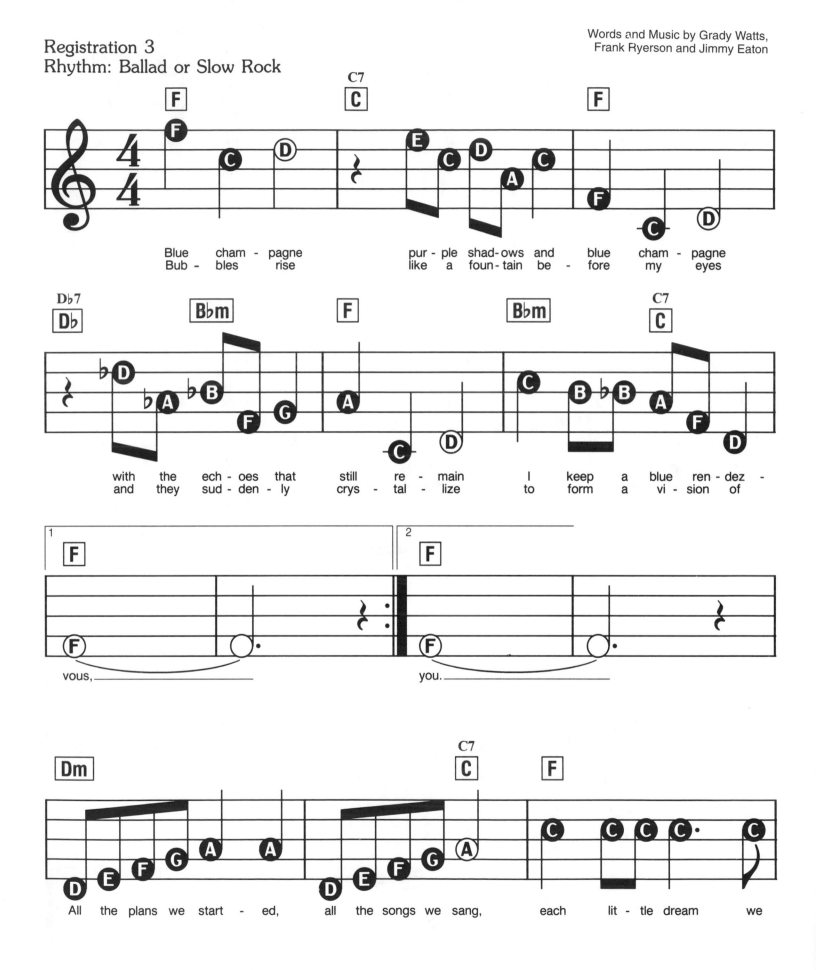

Blue cham - pagne   pur - ple shad - ows and   blue cham - pagne
Bub - bles rise   like a foun - tain be - fore my eyes

with the ech - oes that   still re - main   I keep a blue ren - dez -
and they sud - den - ly   crys - tal - lize   to form a vi - sion of

vous,   you.

All the plans we start - ed,   all the songs we sang,   each lit - tle dream we

19

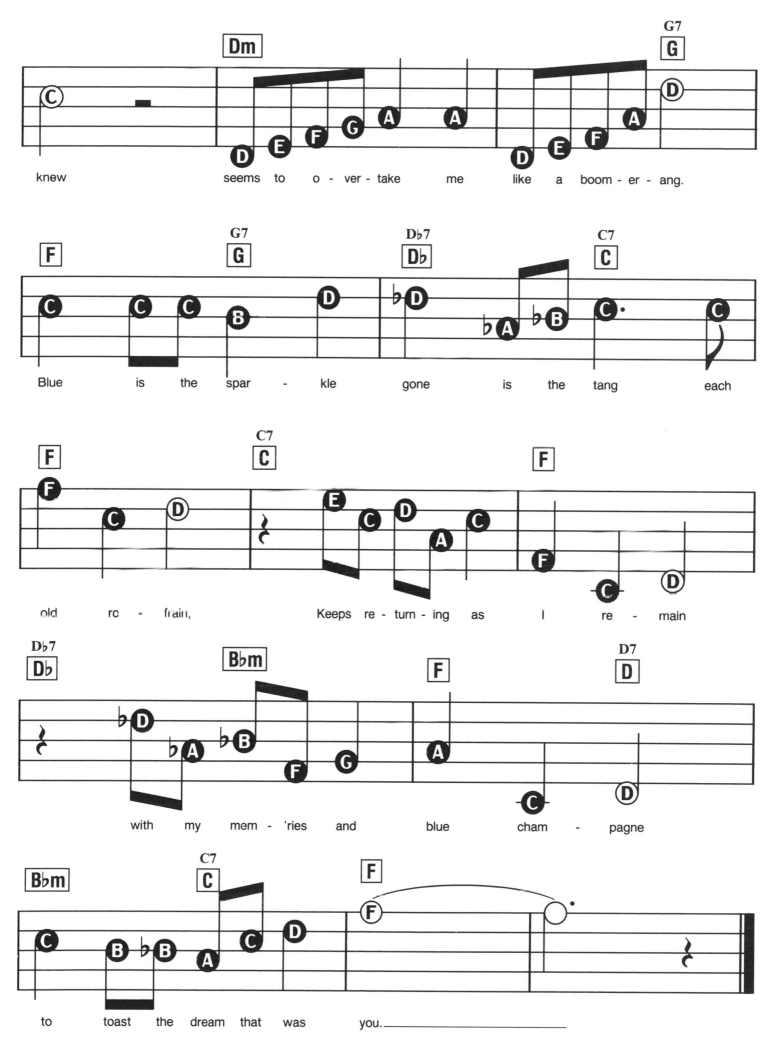

Boo-Hoo

Registration 10
Rhythm: Swing or Jazz

Words and Music by Edward Heyman,
Carmen Lombardo and John Jacob Loeb

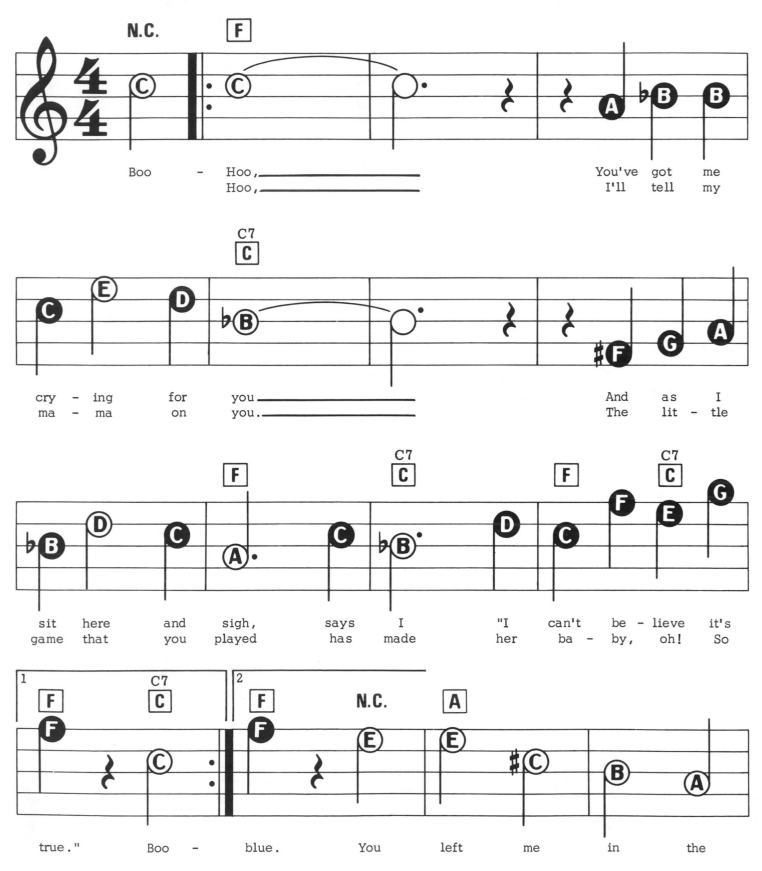

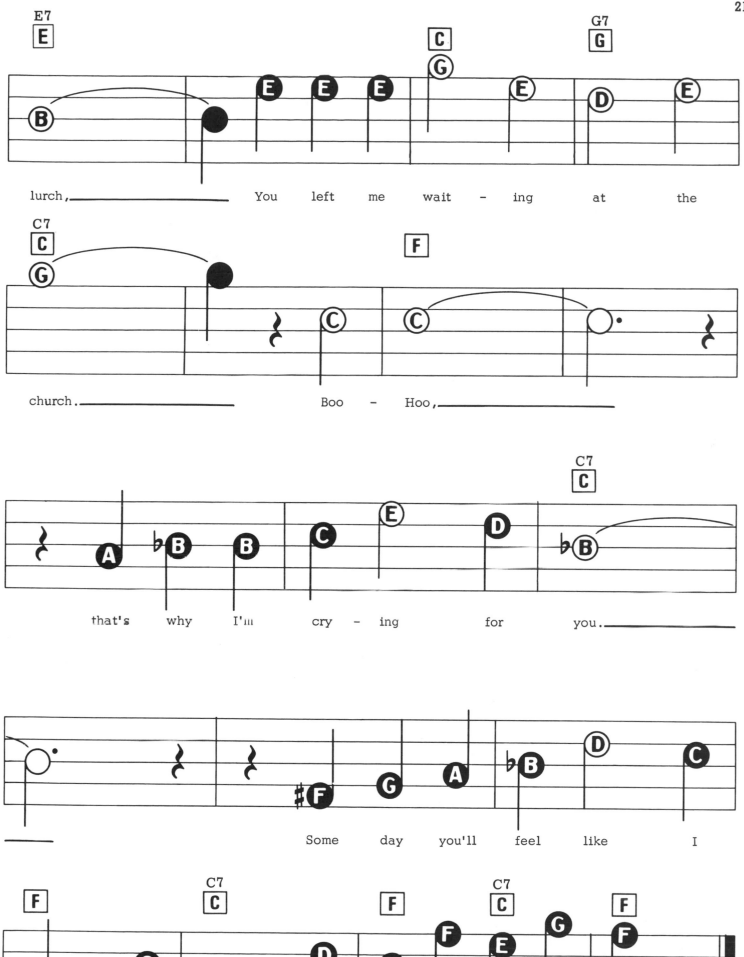

lurch,_____ You left me wait - ing at the church._____ Boo - Hoo,_____ that's why I'm cry - ing for you._____

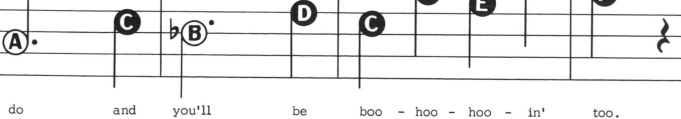

do and you'll be boo - hoo - hoo - in' too.

Bugle Call Rag

Registration 5
Rhythm: Rhythm 'n' Blues or Fox Trot

By Jack Pettis,
Billy Meyers and Elmer Schoebel

bold. You're bound to   Hold me ba - by;   Let's syn - co - pate

to   that   blue   mel - o - dy;   Just   hes - i - tate

while   a   break   they take   Shh!   While   we're   danc - ing

please   hold   me tight;   step   live - ly don't   lag.

Swing   a - long   to   that   Bu - gle Call   Rag. _____

Bye Bye Blackbird
from PETE KELLY'S BLUES

Registration 2
Rhythm: Fox Trot or Swing

Words by Mort Dixon
Music by Ray Henderson

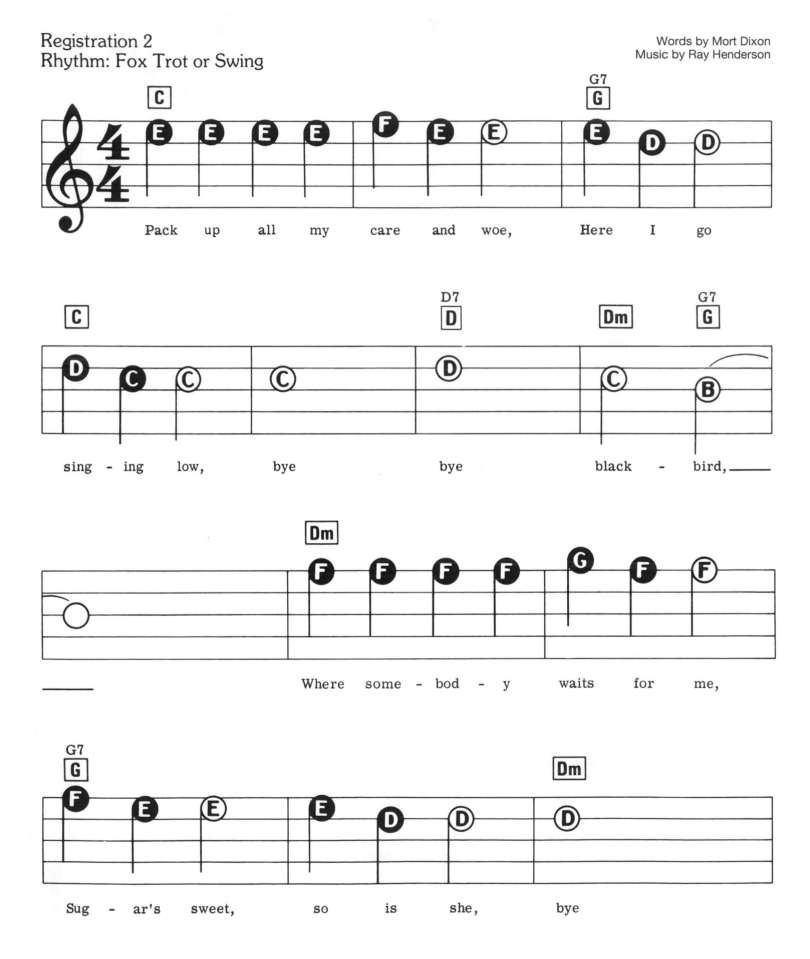

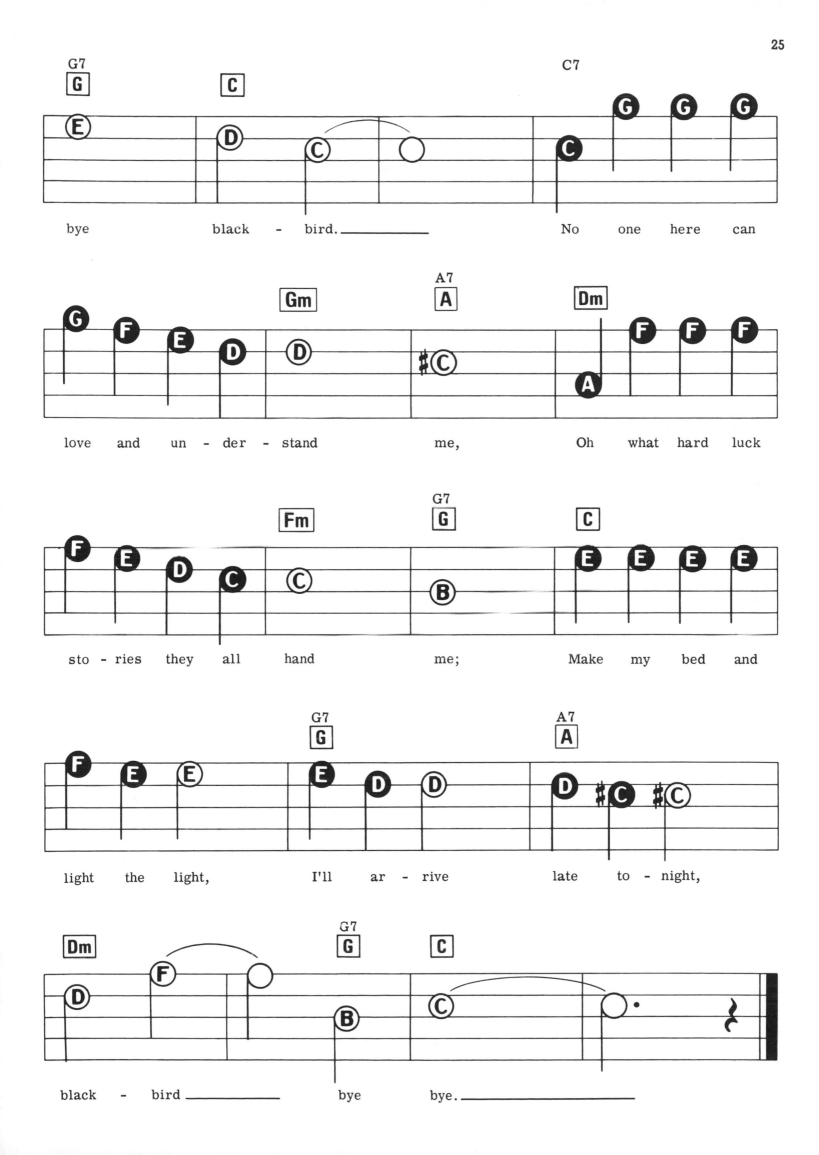

Caldonia
(What Makes Your Big Head So Hard?)

Registration 1
Rhythm: Swing

Words and Music by
Fleecie Moore

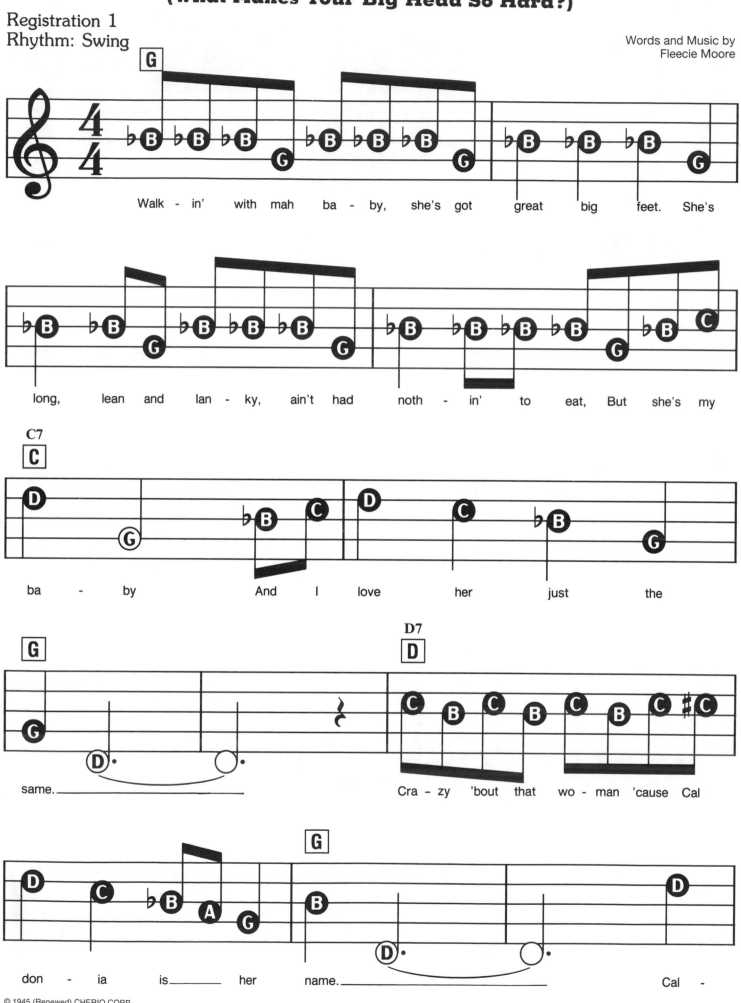

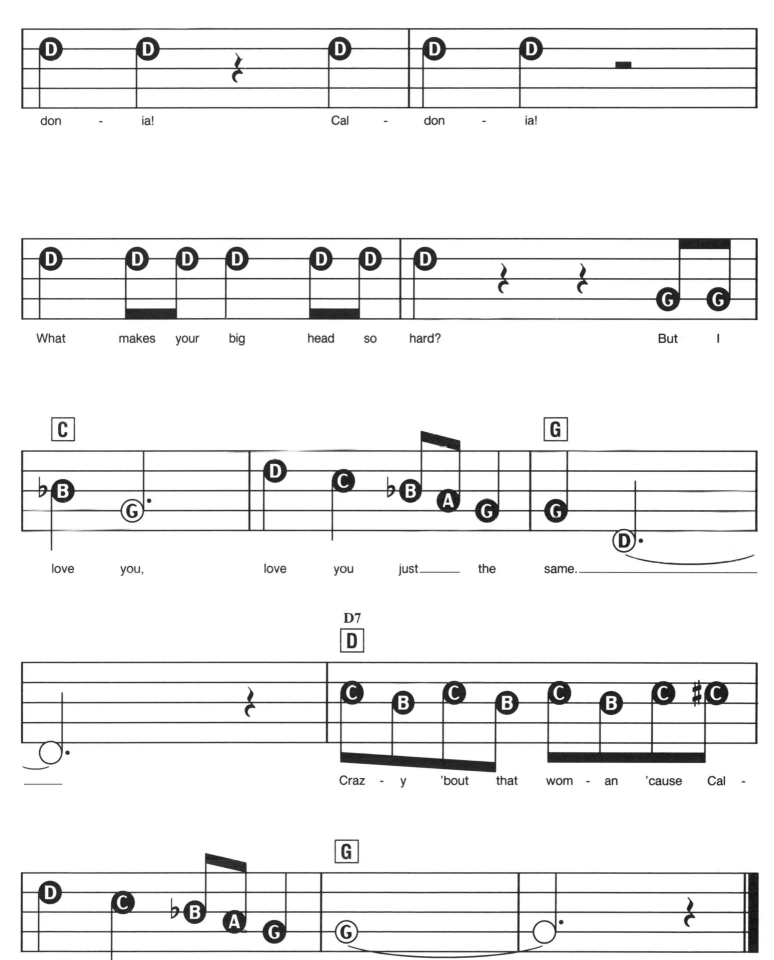

Candy

Registration 4
Rhythm: Fox Trot or Swing

By Alex Kramer,
Joan Whitney and Mack David

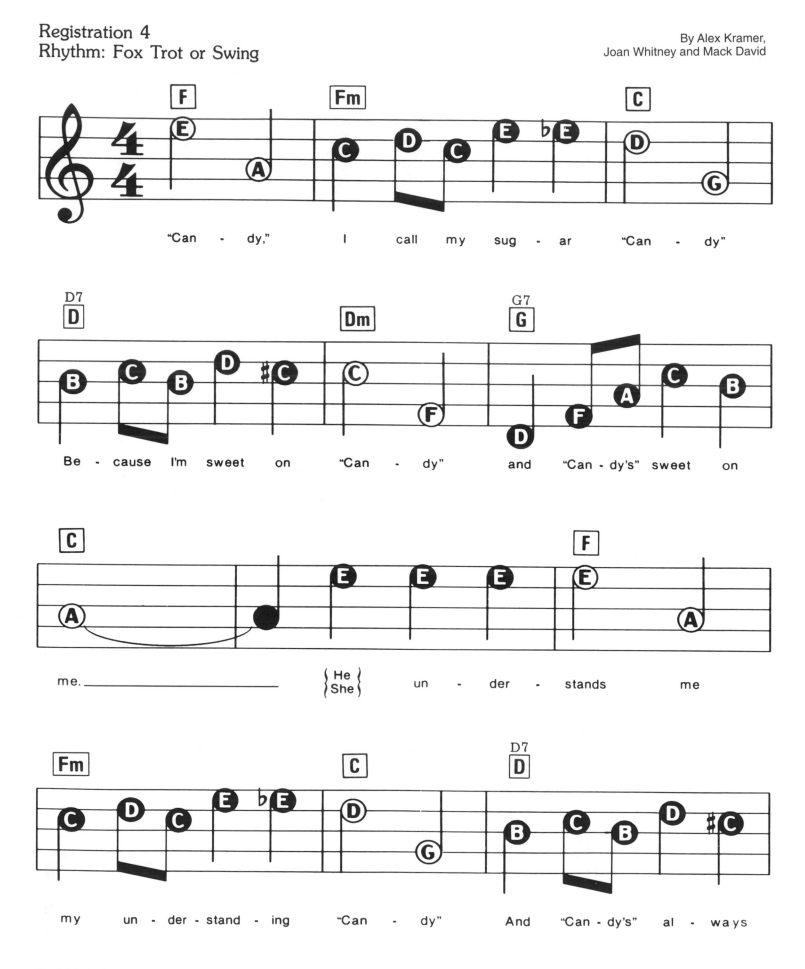

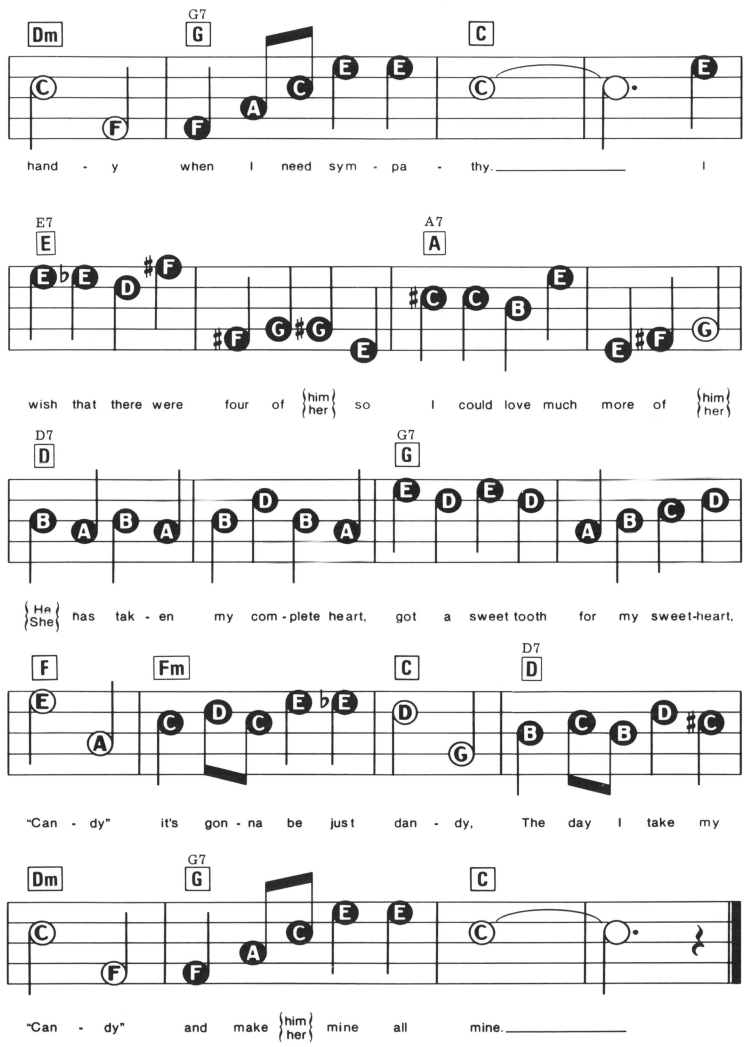

The Continental
from THE GAY DIVORCEE

Registration 5
Rhythm: Samba or Latin

Words by Con Conrad
Music by Herbert Magidson

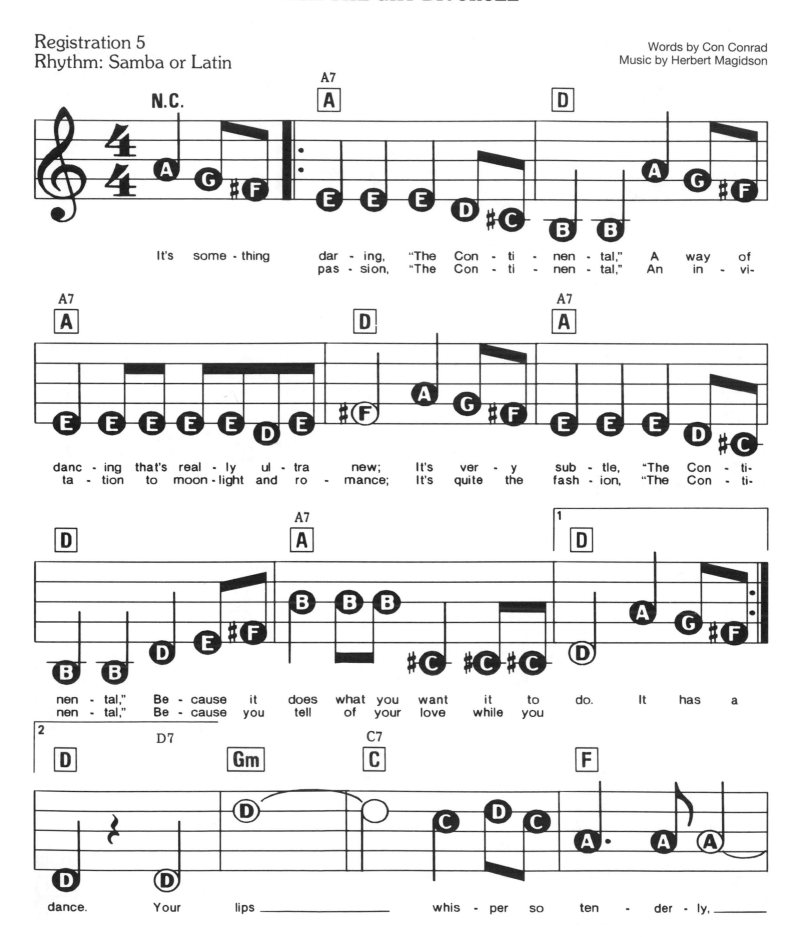

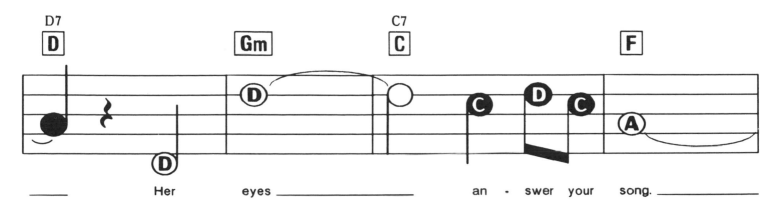

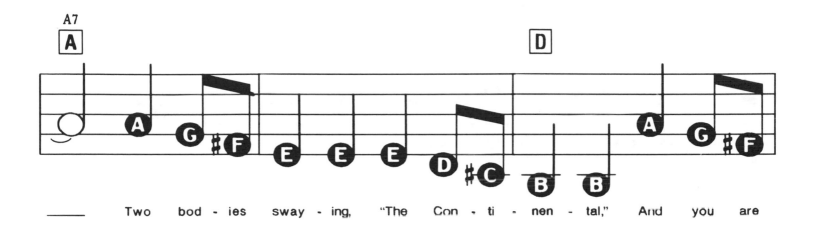

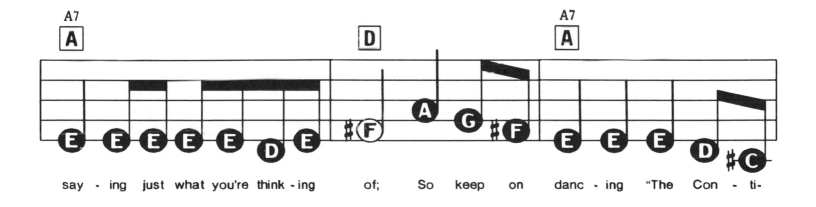

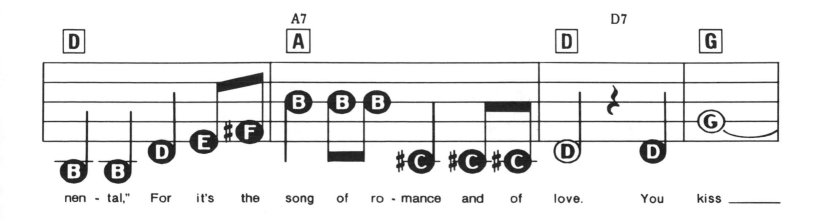

32

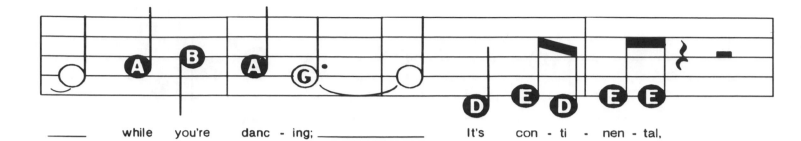

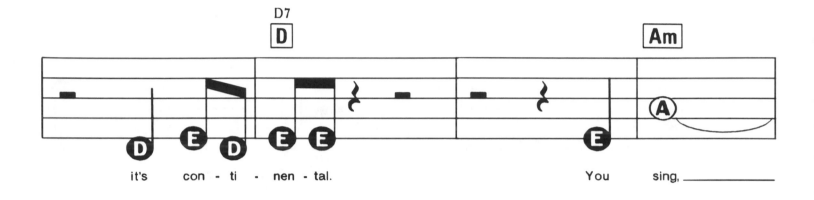

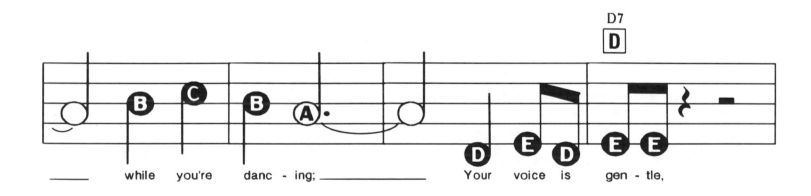

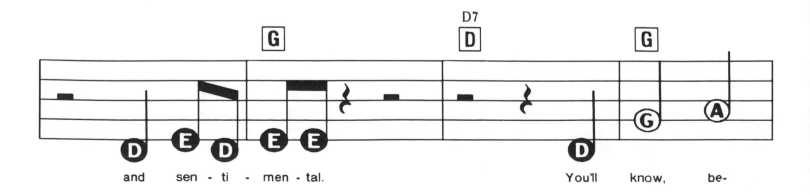

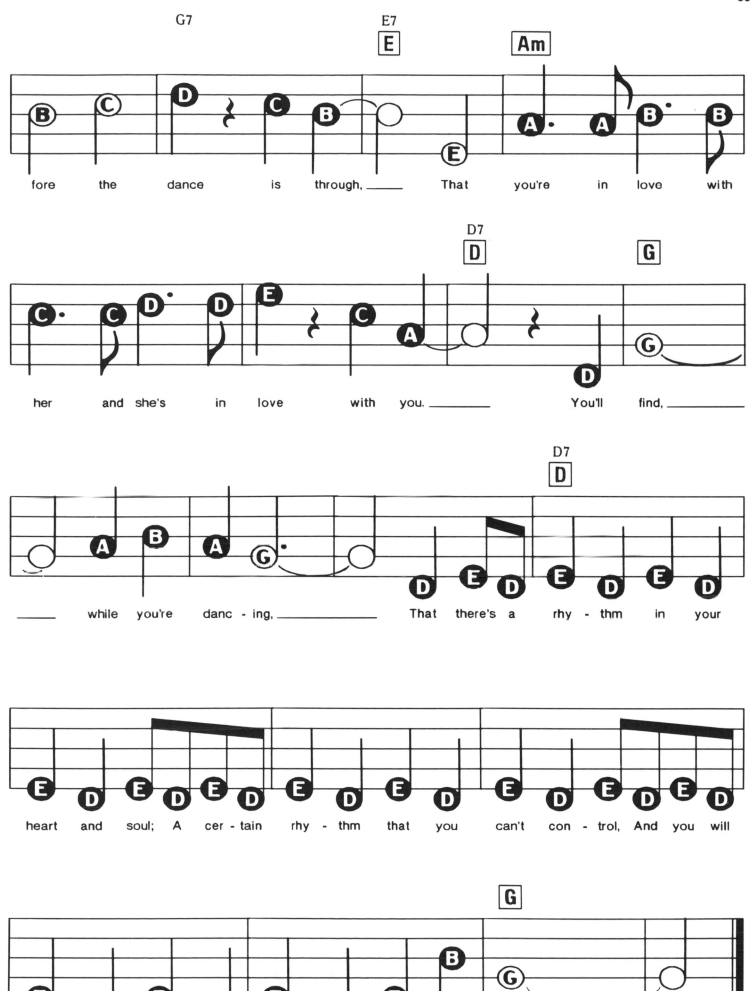

Cherry Pink And Apple Blossom White

Registration 9
Rhythm: Latin or Rhumba

French Words by Jacques Larue
English Words by Mack David
Music by Louiguy

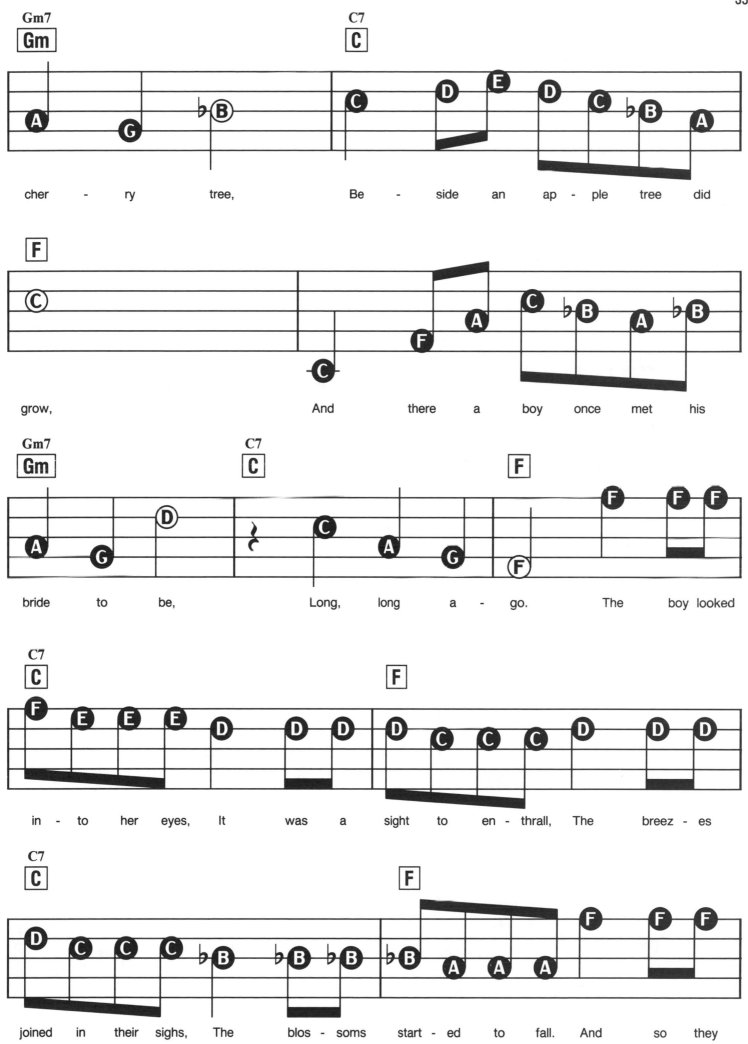

35

36

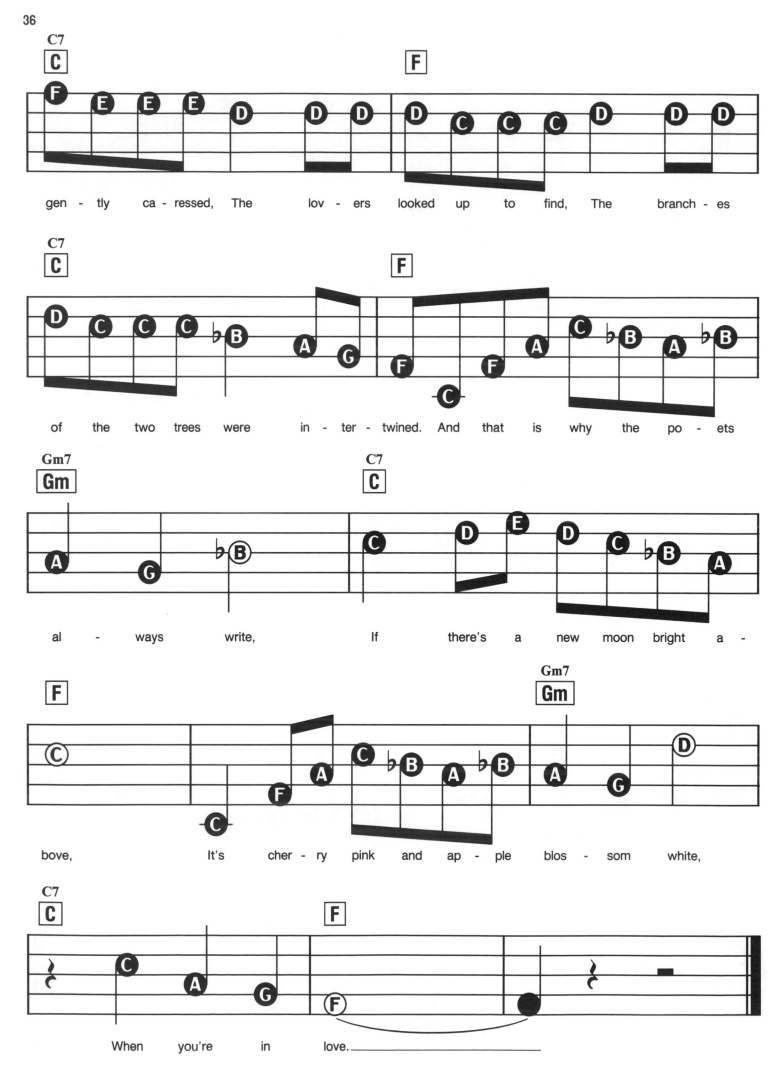

Daddy

Registration 5
Rhythm: Fox Trot or Swing

Words and Music by
Bob Troup

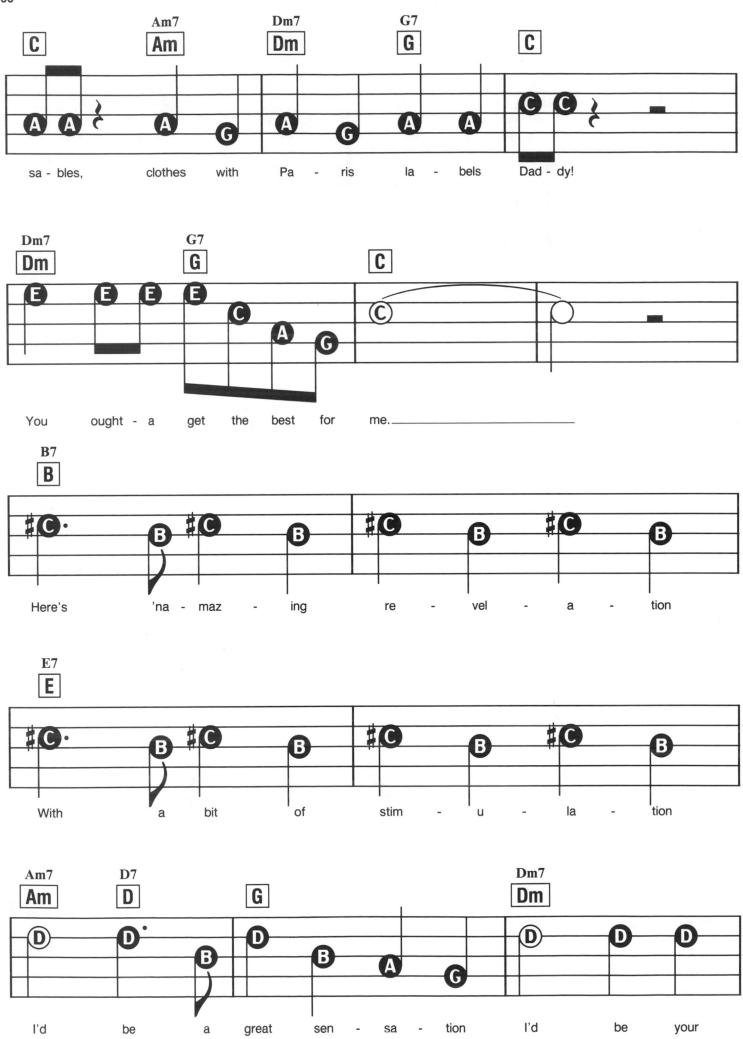

Don't Get Around Much Anymore

Registration 5
Rhythm: Fox Trot or Swing

Words and Music by Bob Russell
and Duke Ellington

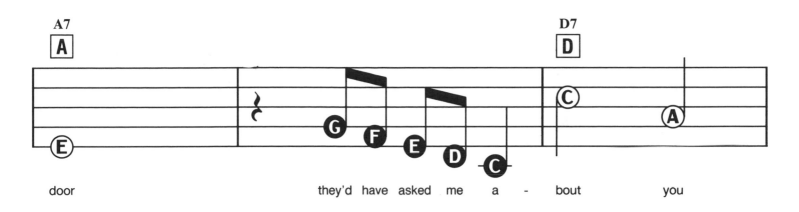

door   they'd have asked me a - bout you

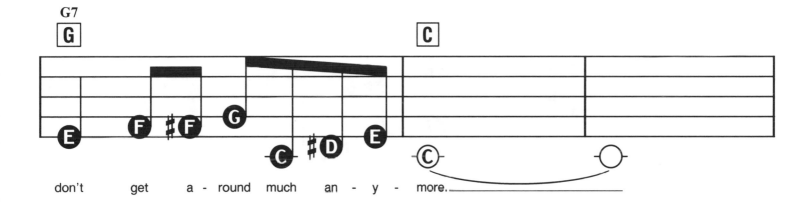

don't   get   a - round much an - y - more._____

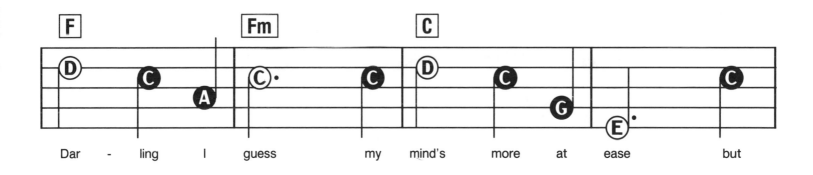

Dar - ling   I   guess   my   mind's   more   at   ease   but

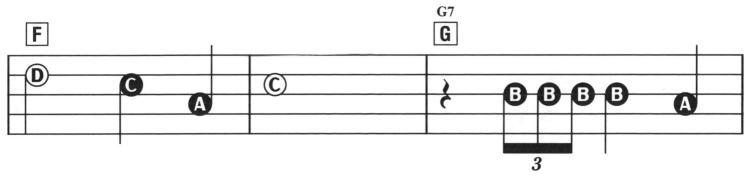

nev - er - the - less   why stir up mem - o -

42

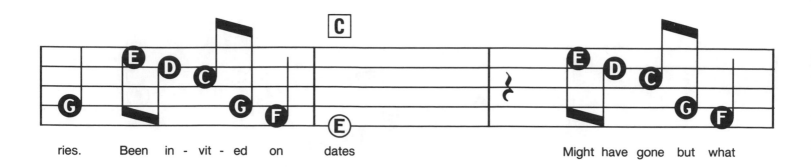

ries. Been in - vit - ed on dates   Might have gone but what

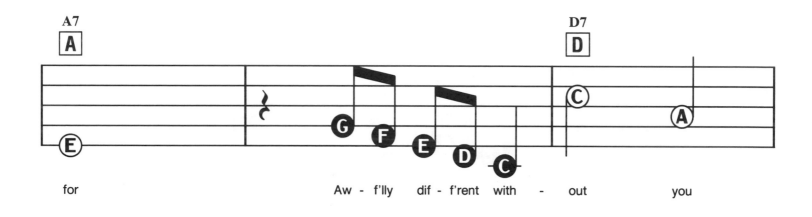

A7   D7

for   Aw - f'lly dif - f'rent with - out   you

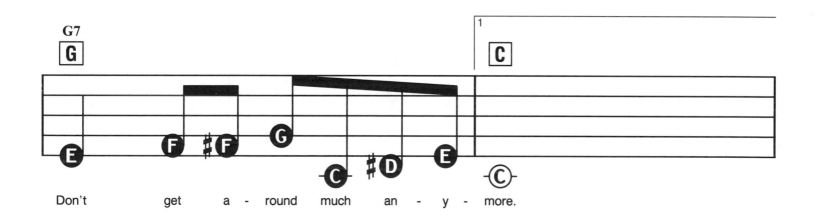

G7   1

Don't   get a - round much an - y - more.

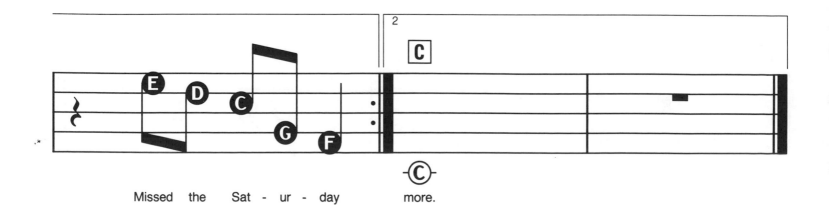

                                       2

Missed the Sat - ur - day   more.

In The Mood

Registration 8
Rhythm: Swing

By Joe Garland

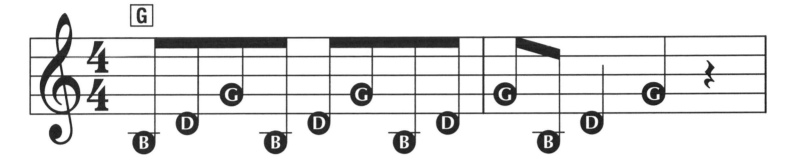

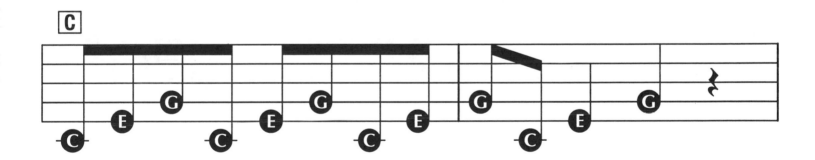

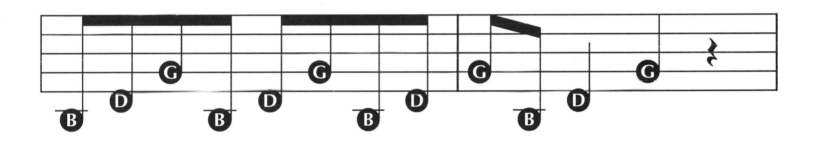

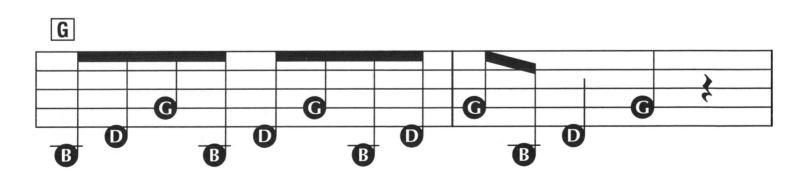

44

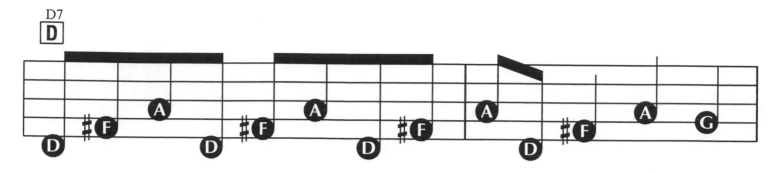

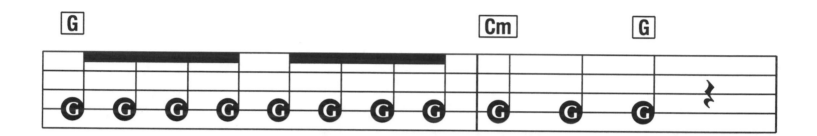

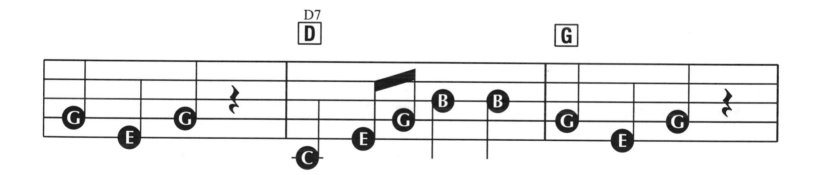

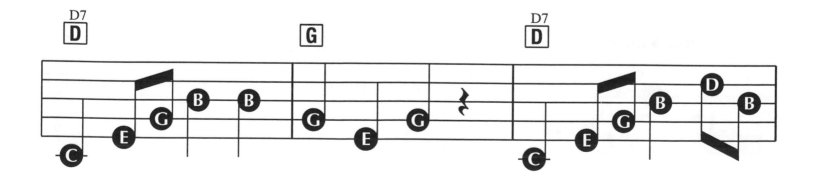

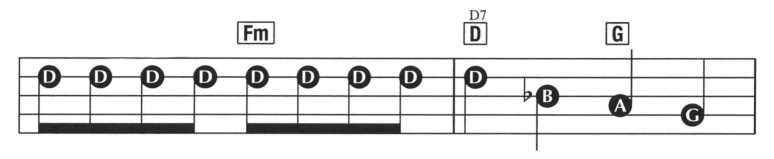

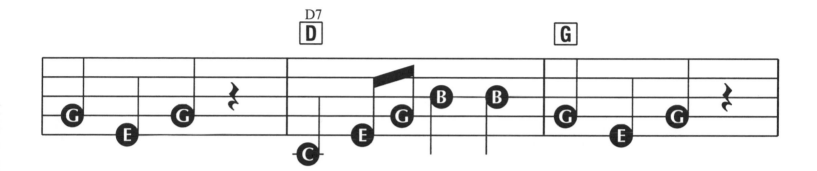

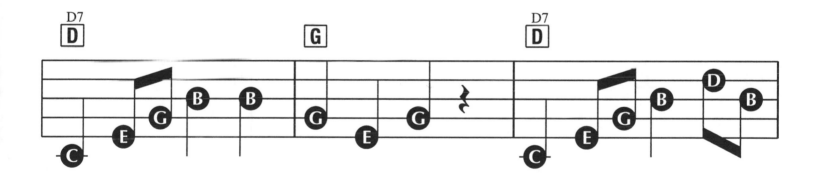

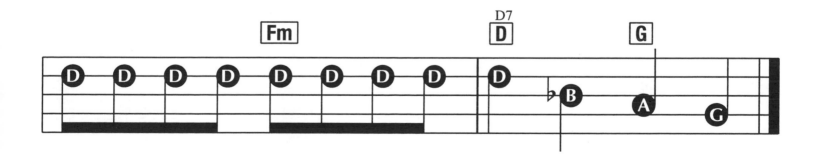

Five Foot Two, Eyes of Blue
(Has Anybody Seen My Girl?)

Registration 9
Rhythm: Fox Trot

Words by Joe Young and Sam Lewis
Music by Ray Henderson

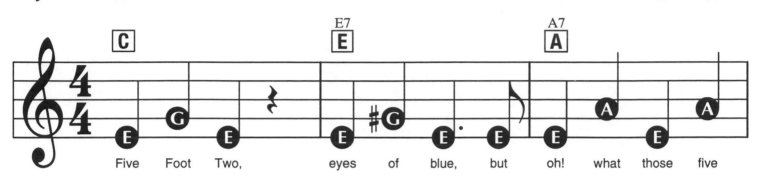

Five Foot Two, eyes of blue, but oh! what those five

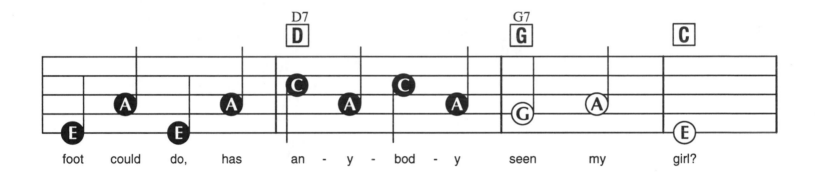

foot could do, has an - y - bod - y seen my girl?

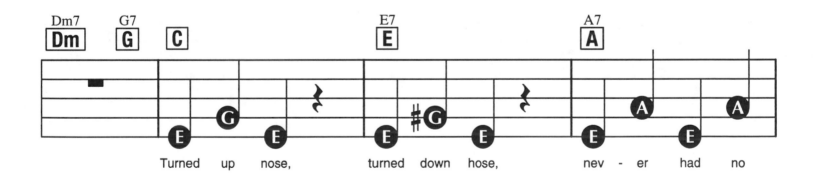

Turned up nose, turned down hose, nev - er had no

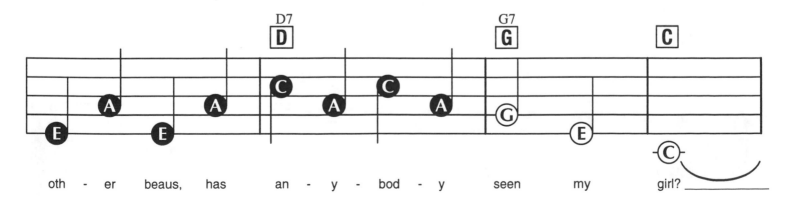

oth - er beaus, has an - y - bod - y seen my girl? _____

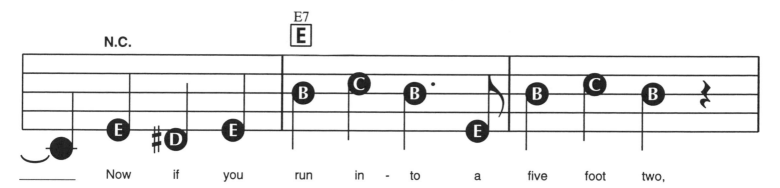

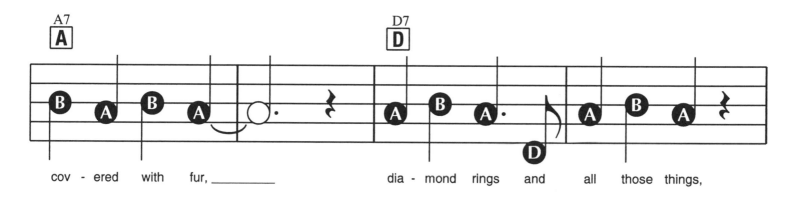

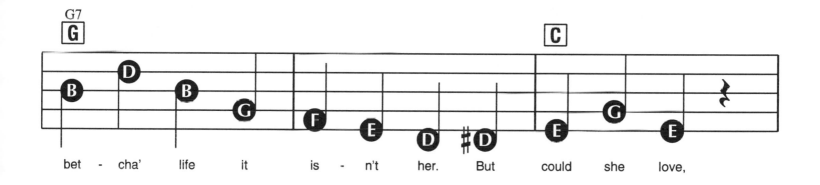

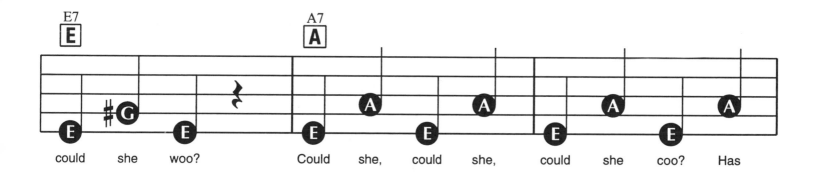

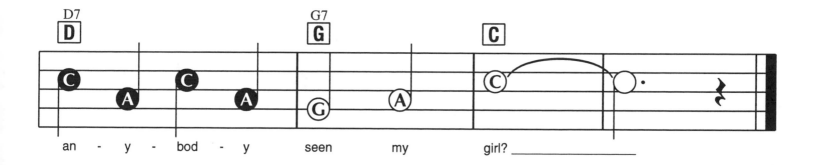

(I Love You)
For Sentimental Reasons

Registration 1
Rhythm: Fox Trot or Swing

Words by Deek Watson
Music by William Best

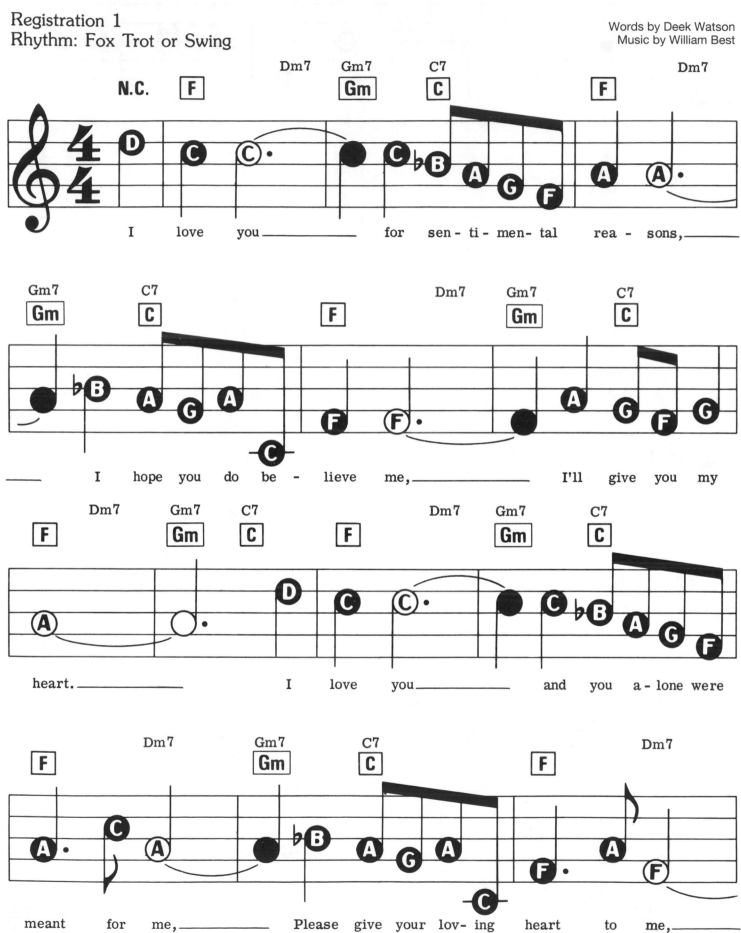

MCA Music Publishing

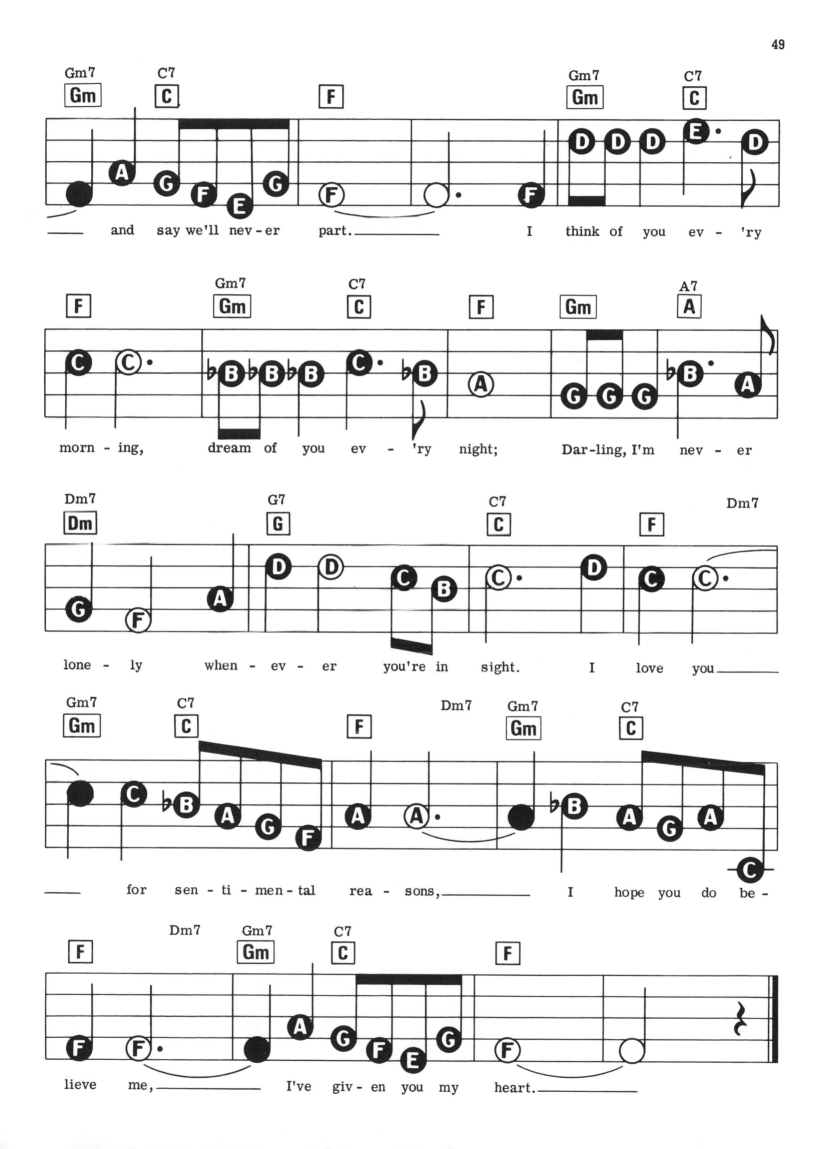

Harlem Nocturne

Registration 2
Rhythm: Swing or Jazz

Words by Dick Rogers
Music by Earle Hagen

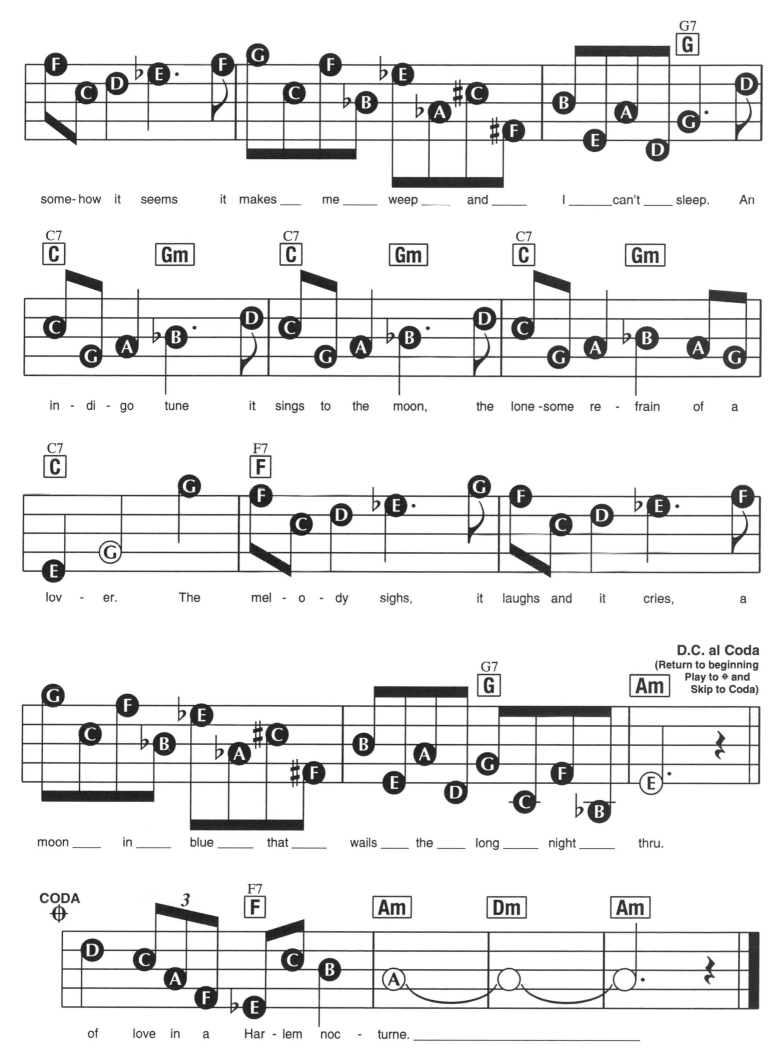

I Can't Give You Anything But Love

from BLACKBIRDS OF 1928

Registration 5
Rhythm: Swing or Jazz

Words by Dorothy Fields
Music by Jimmy McHugh

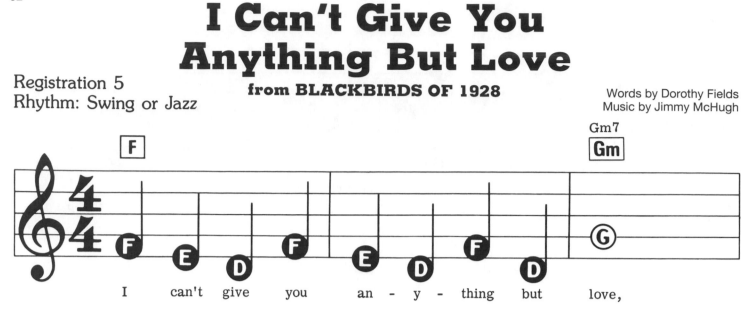

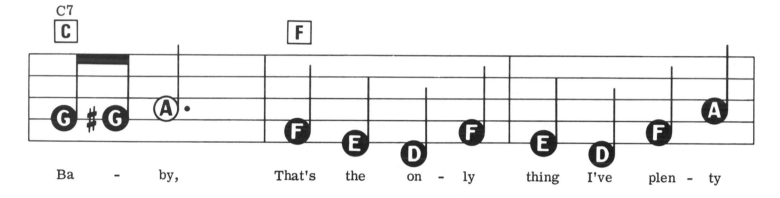

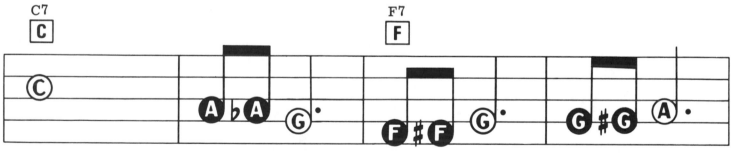

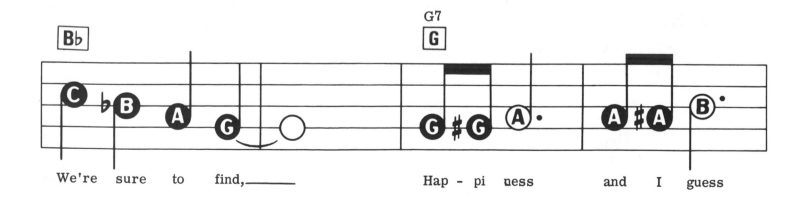

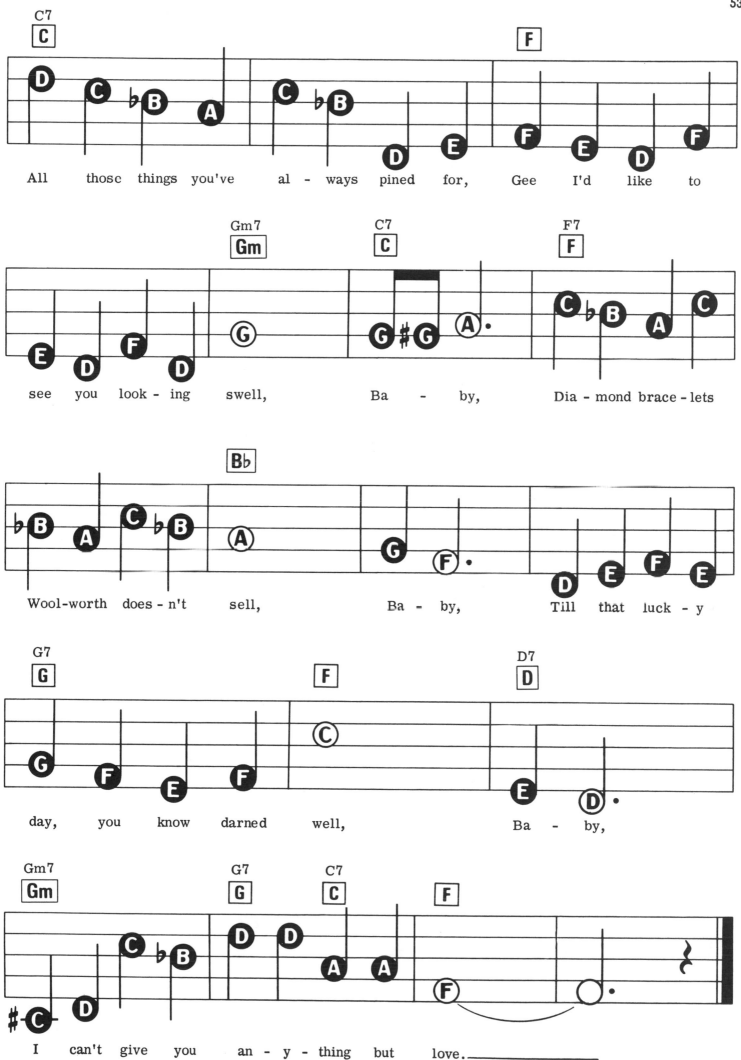

I'll Never Smile Again

Registration 9
Rhythm: Swing or Fox Trot

Words and Music by
Ruth Lowe

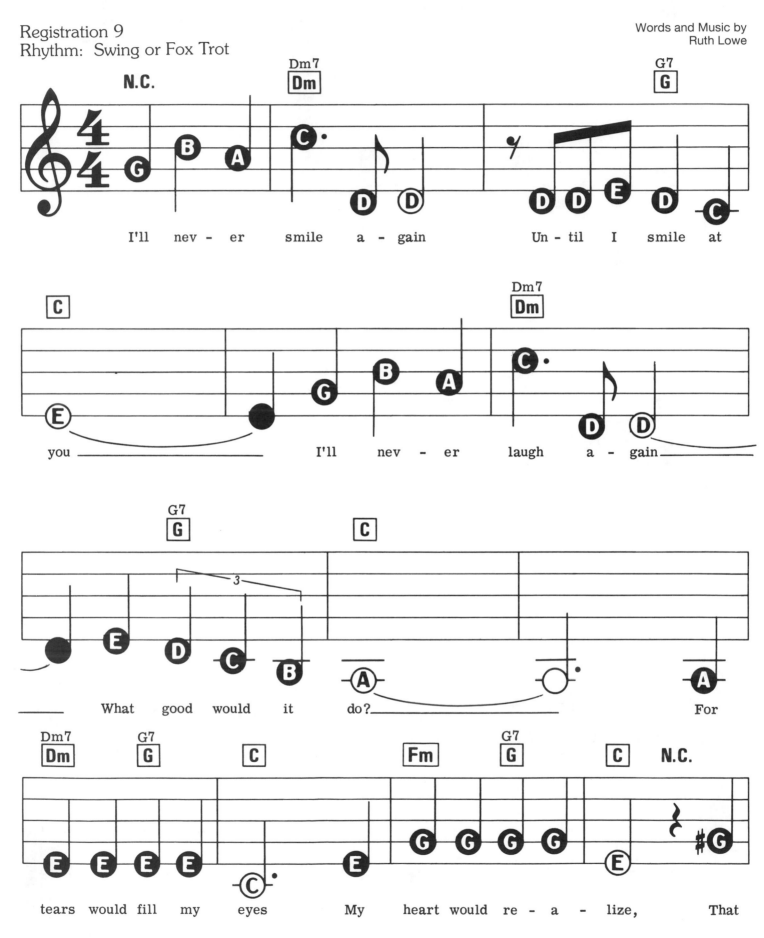

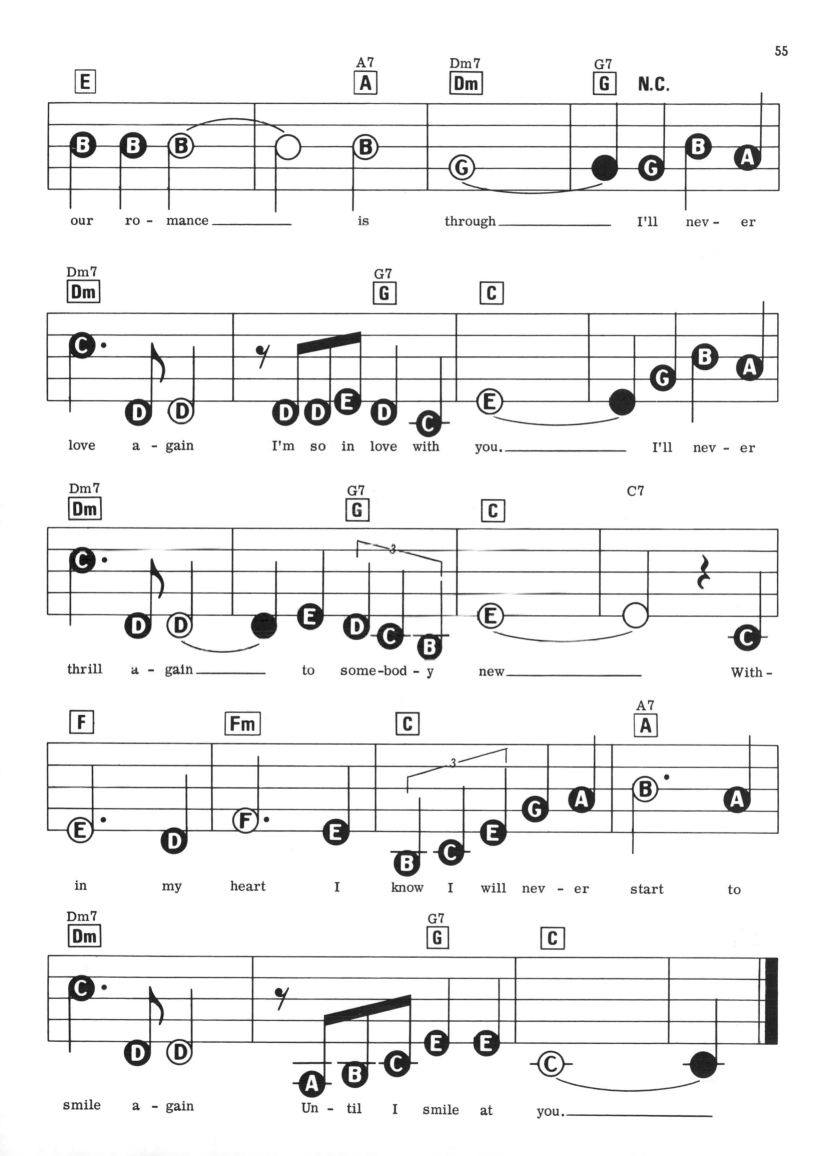

I'll Remember April

Registration 3
Rhythm: Swing

Words and Music by Don Raye,
Gene De Paul and Pat Johnson

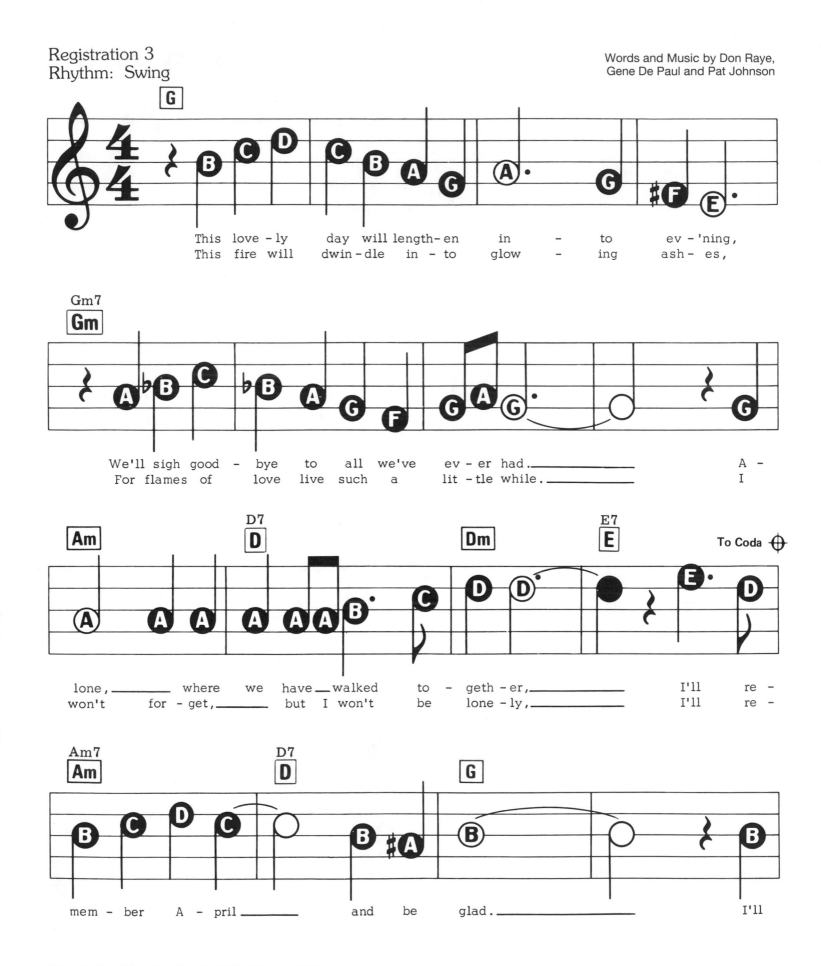

MCA Music Publishing

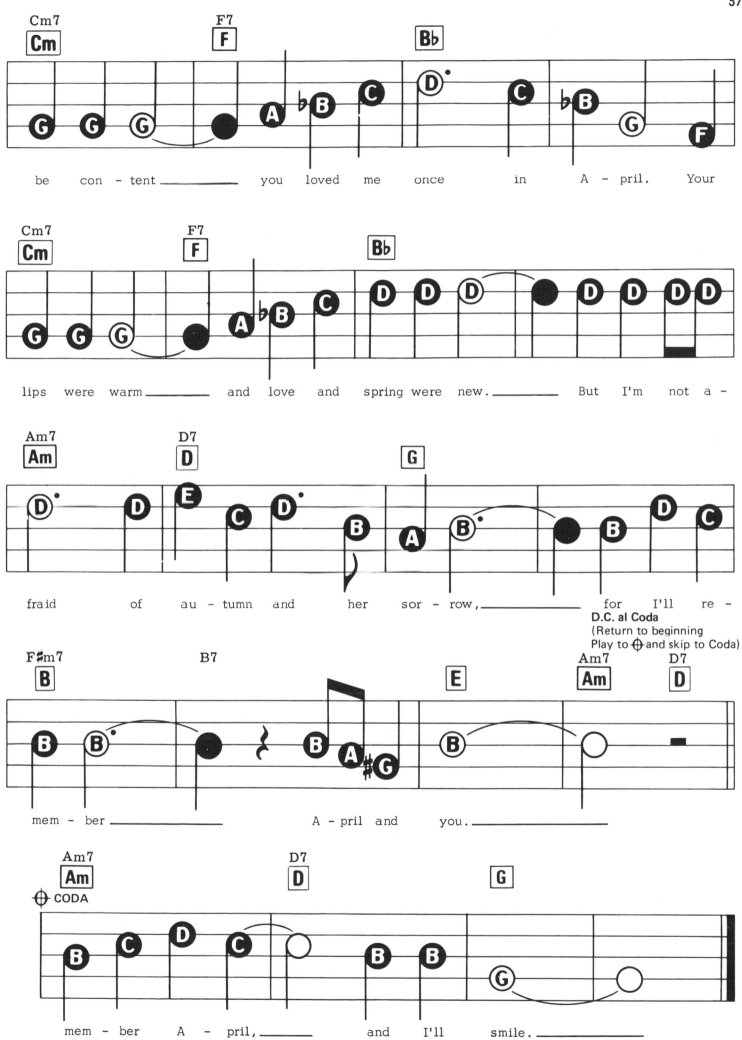

I'm Sitting On Top Of The World

Registration 3
Rhythm: Fox Trot

Words by Sam M. Lewis and Joe Young
Music by Ray Henderson

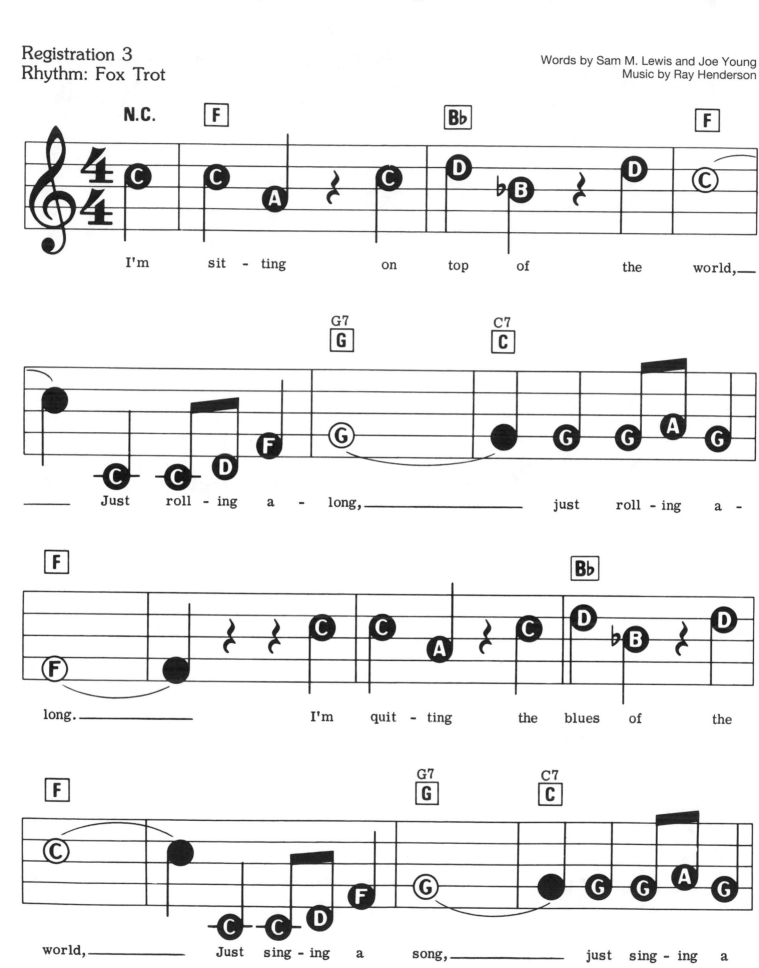

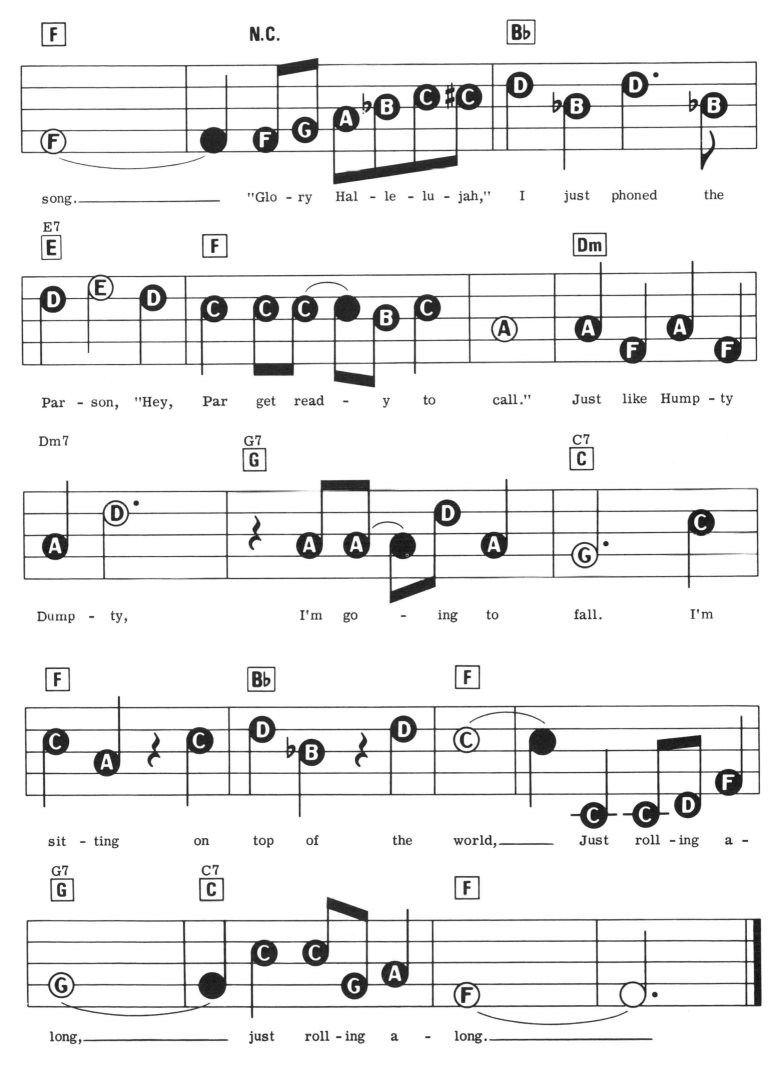

In A Little Spanish Town
('Twas On A Night Like This)

Registration 3
Rhythm: Waltz

Words by Sam M. Lewis and Joe Young
Music by Mabel Wayne

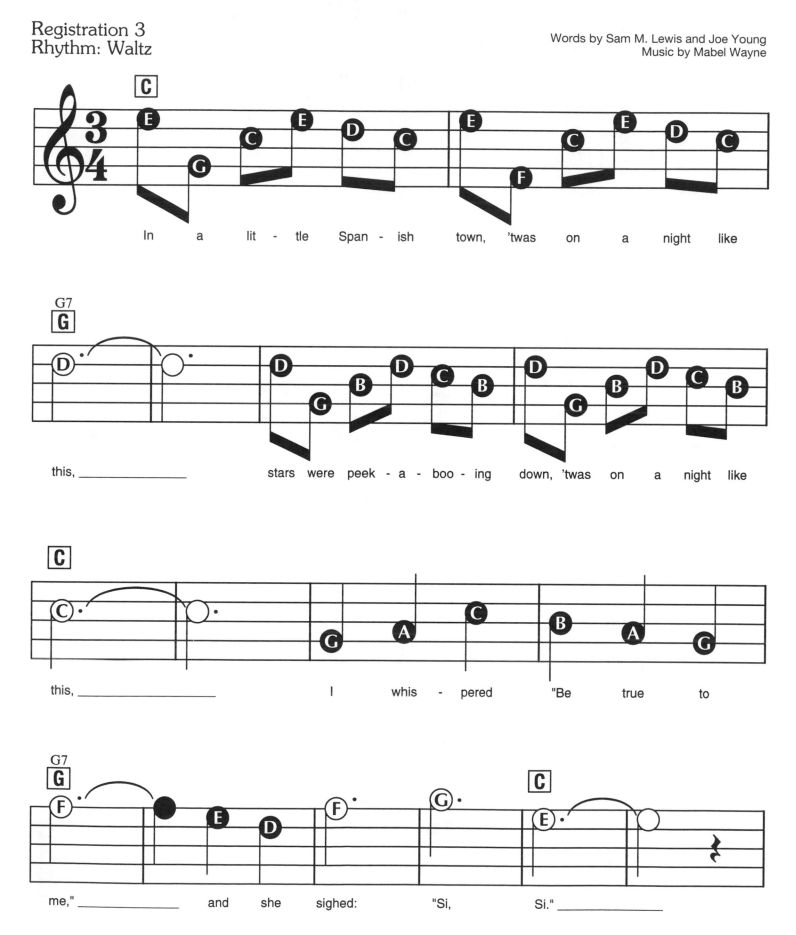

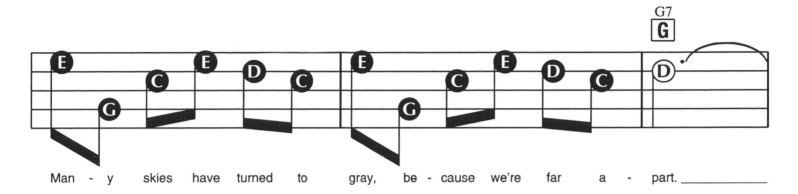

Man - y skies have turned to gray, be - cause we're far a - part. _____

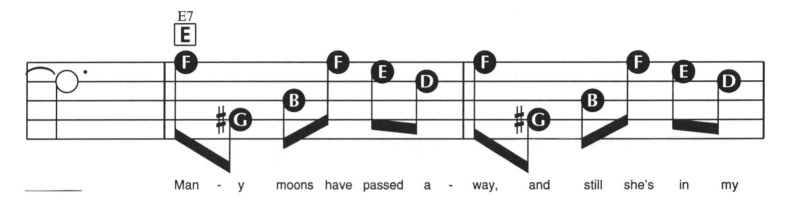

_____ Man - y moons have passed a - way, and still she's in my

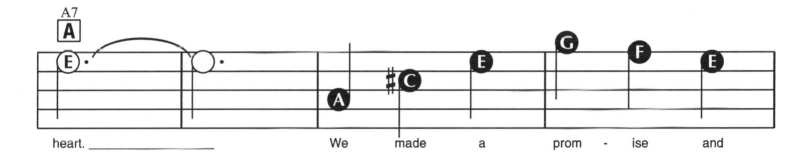

heart. _____ We made a prom - ise and

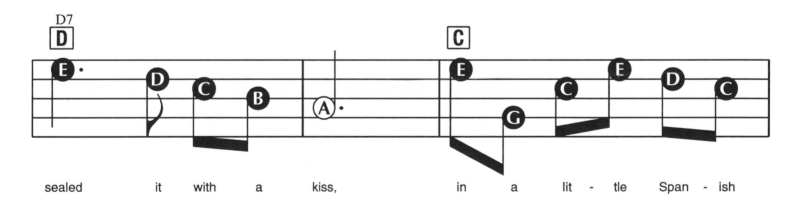

sealed it with a kiss, in a lit - tle Span - ish

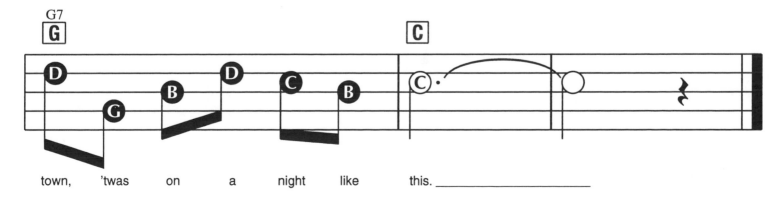

town, 'twas on a night like this. _____

Don't Sit under the Apple Tree
(With Anyone Else but Me)

Registration 2
Rhythm: Swing

Words and Music by Lew Brown,
Sam H. Stept and Charlie Tobias

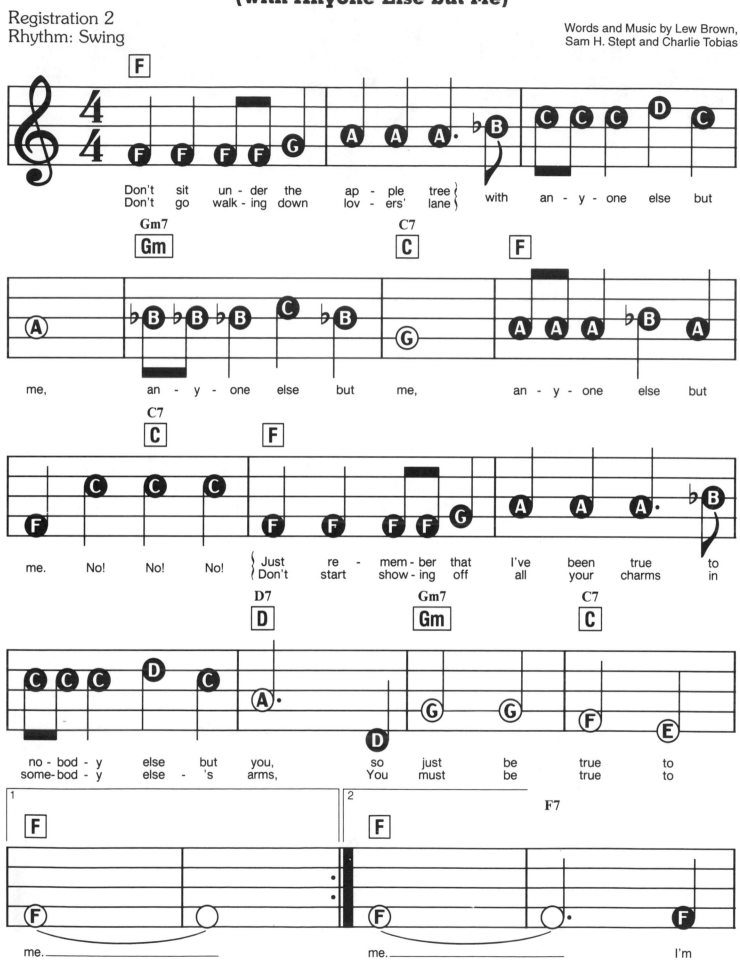

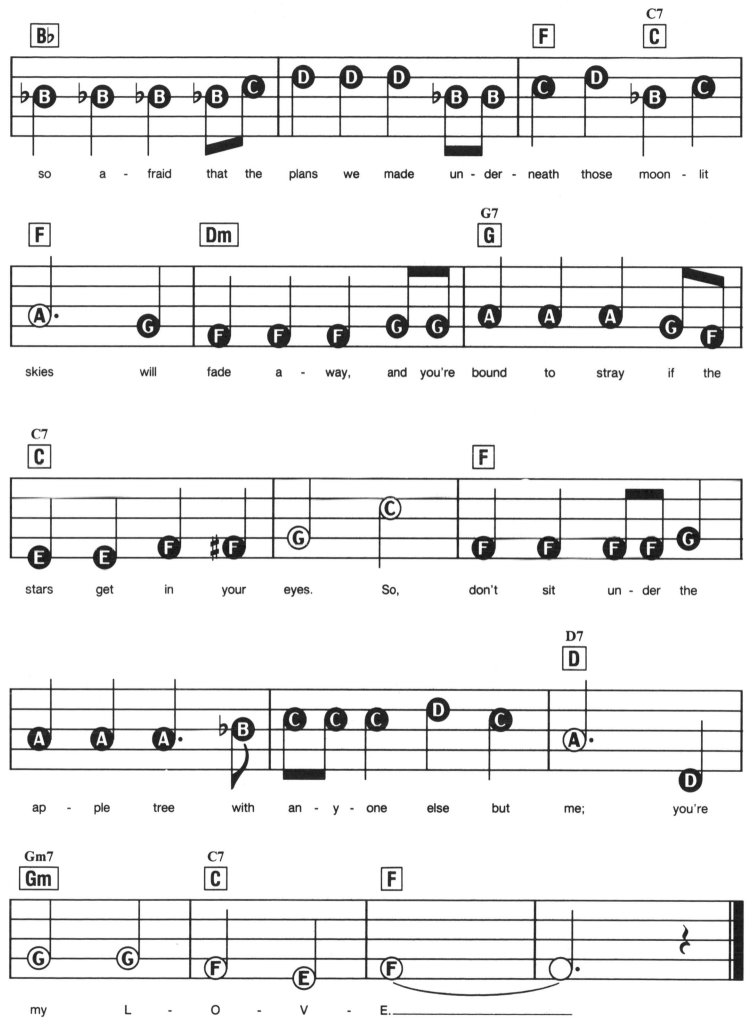

It's A Pity To Say "Goodnight"

Registration 7
Rhythm: Swing or Jazz

Words and Music by
Billy Reid

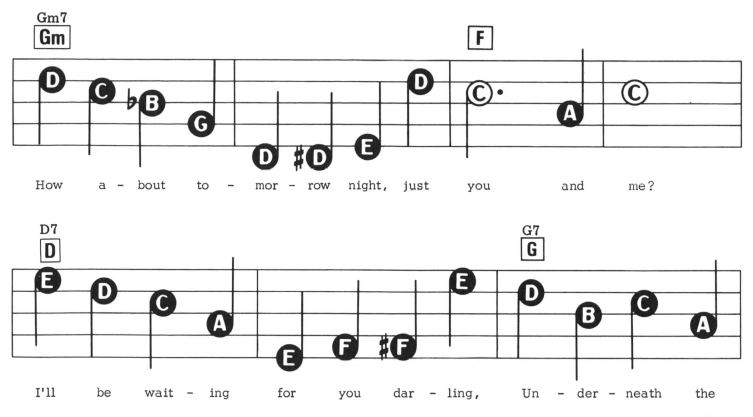

How a - bout to - mor - row night, just you and me?

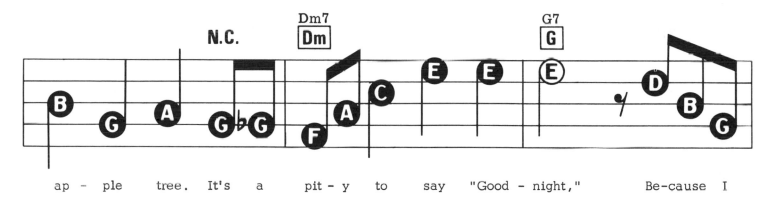

I'll be wait - ing for you dar - ling, Un - der - neath the

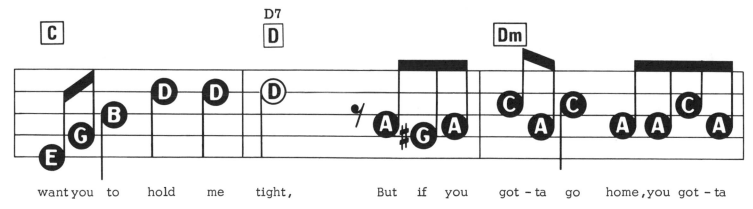

ap - ple tree. It's a pit - y to say "Good - night," Be-cause I

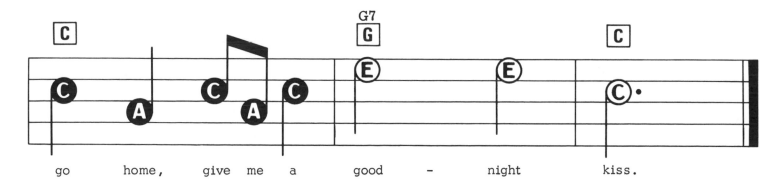

want you to hold me tight, But if you got - ta go home, you got - ta

go home, give me a good - night kiss.

Lazy River

Registration 1
Rhythm: Fox Trot or Swing

Words and Music by Hoagy Carmichael
and Sidney Arodin

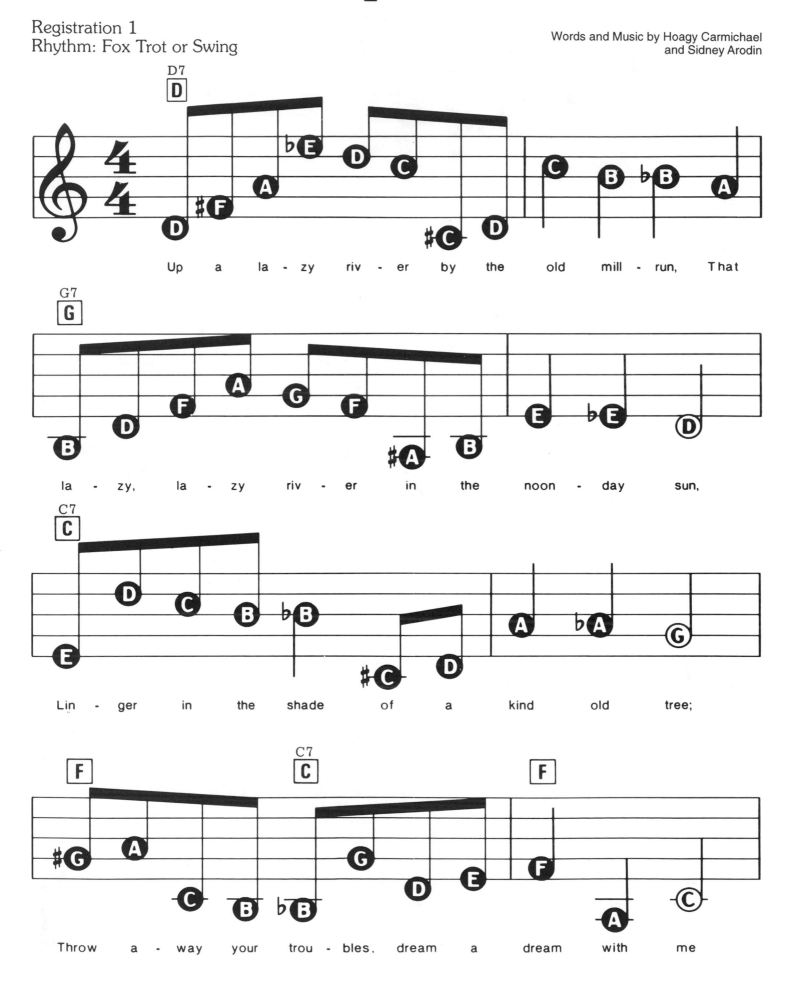

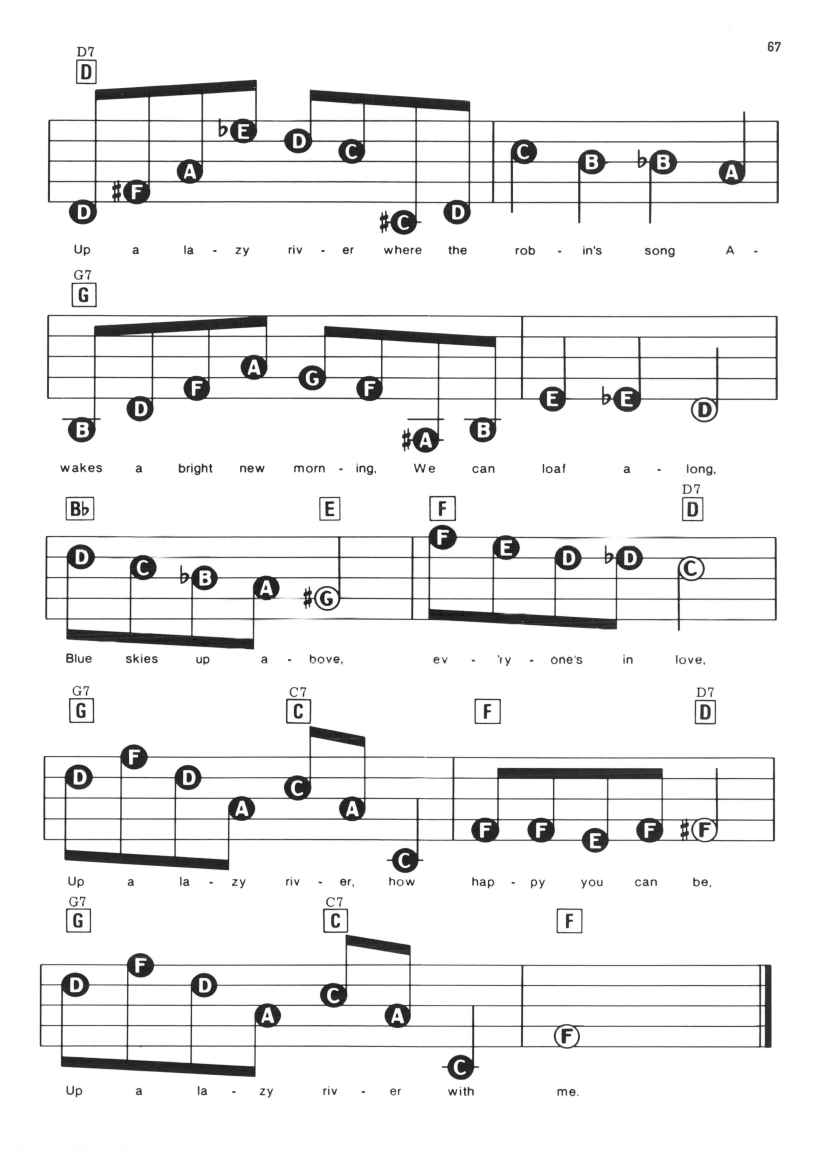

Mood Indigo
from SOPHISTICATED LADIES

Registration 4
Rhythm: Swing or Ballad

Words and Music by Duke Ellington,
Irving Mills and Albany Bigard

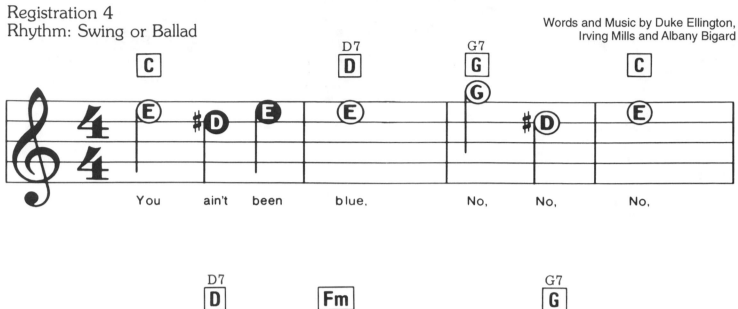

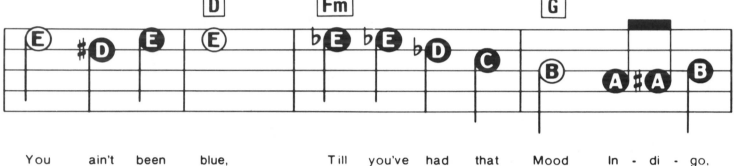

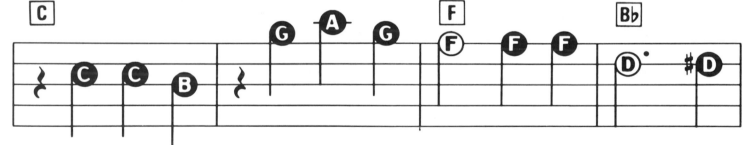

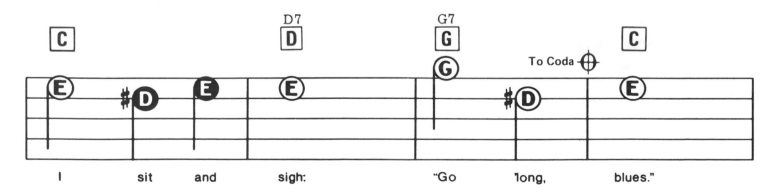

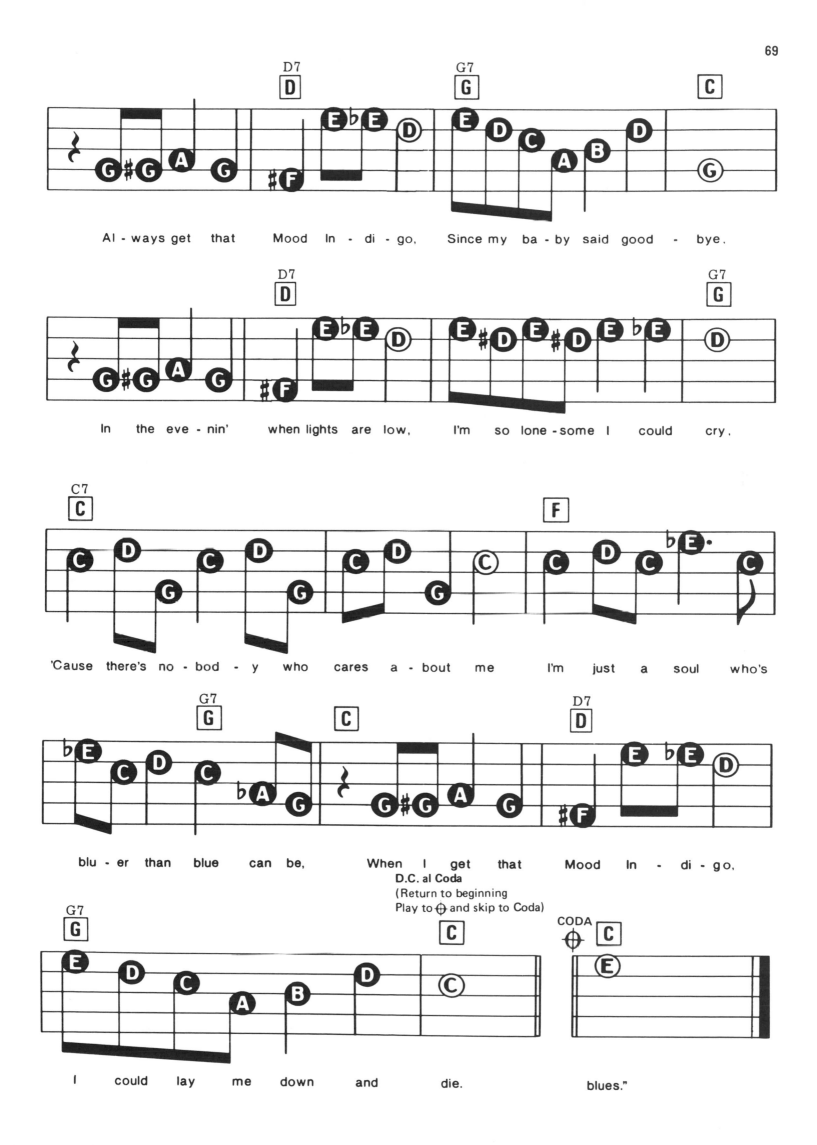

Let There Be Love

Registration 10
Rhythm: Latin

Lyric by Ian Grant
Music by Lionel Rand

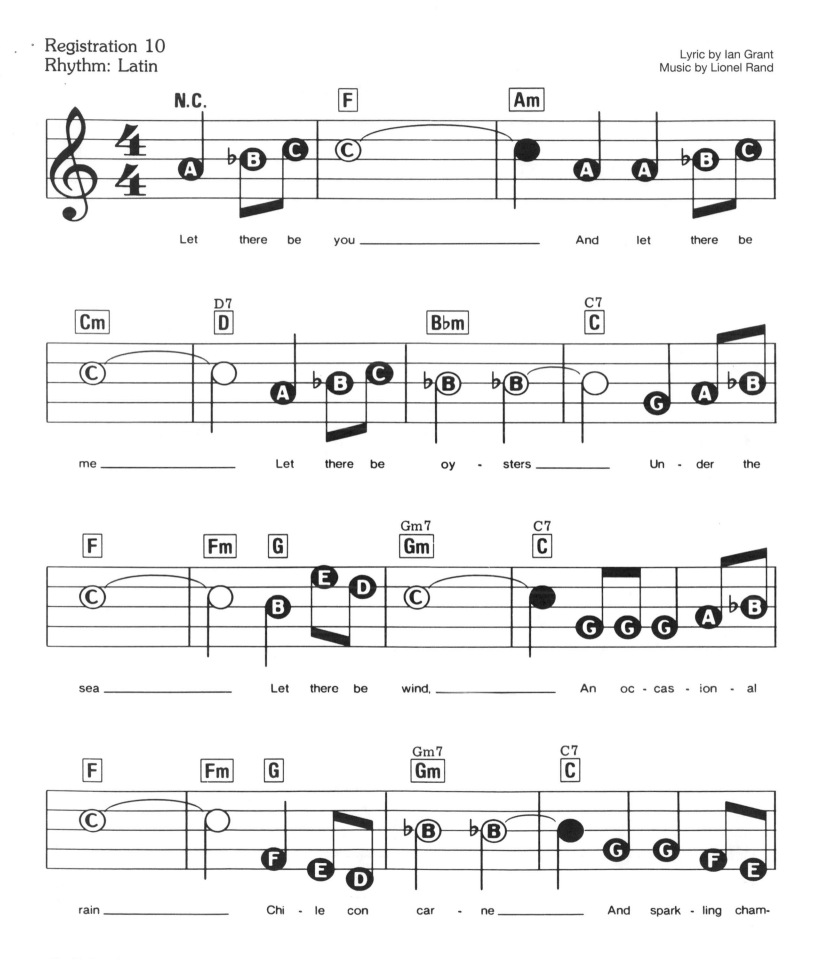

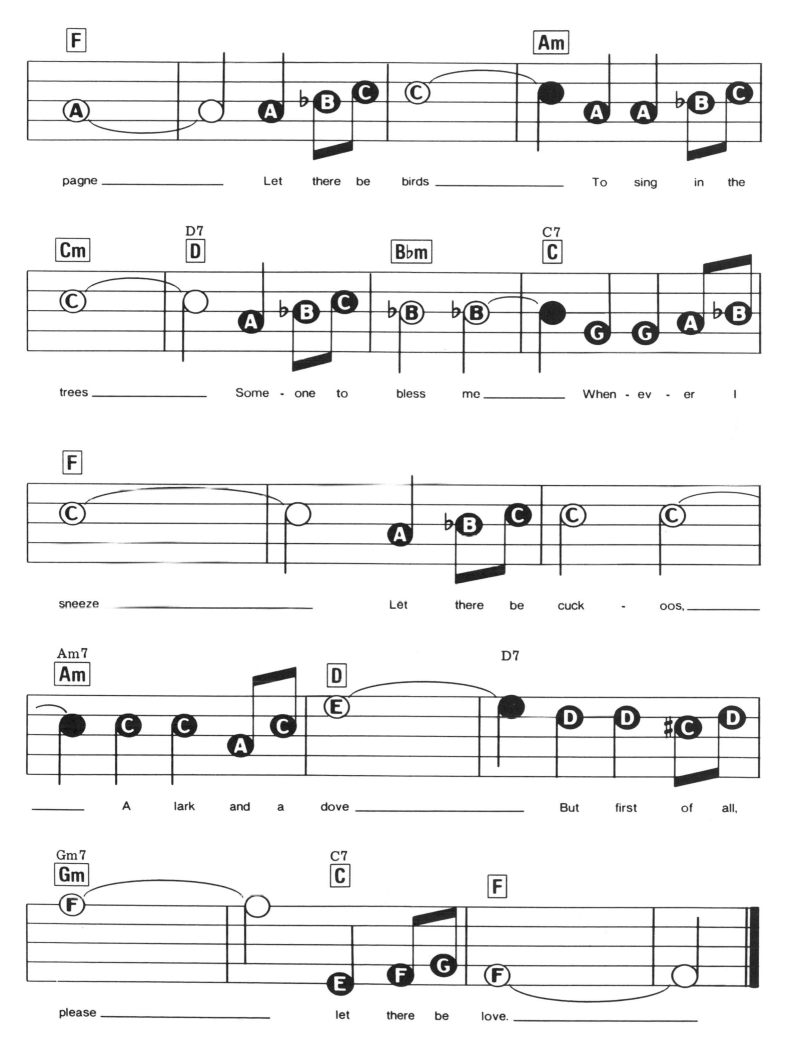

Let's Dance

Registartion 7
Rhythm: Swing or Jazz

Words by Fanny Baldridge
Music by Gregory Stone and Joseph Bonine

73

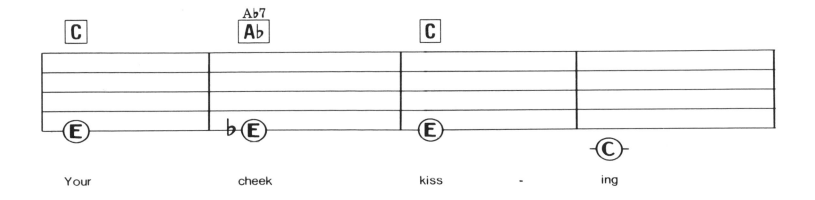

Your cheek kiss - ing

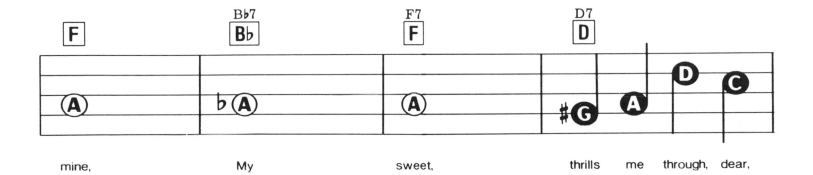

mine, My sweet, thrills me through, dear,

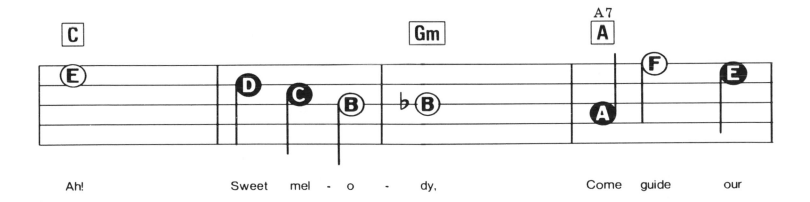

Ah! Sweet mel - o - dy, Come guide our

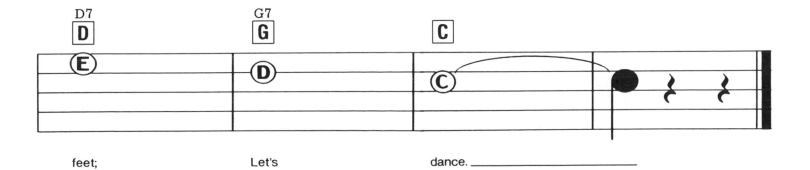

feet; Let's dance. _____

Little Girl

Registration 4
Rhythm: Fox Trot or Swing

Words and Music by Madeline Hyde
and Francis Henry

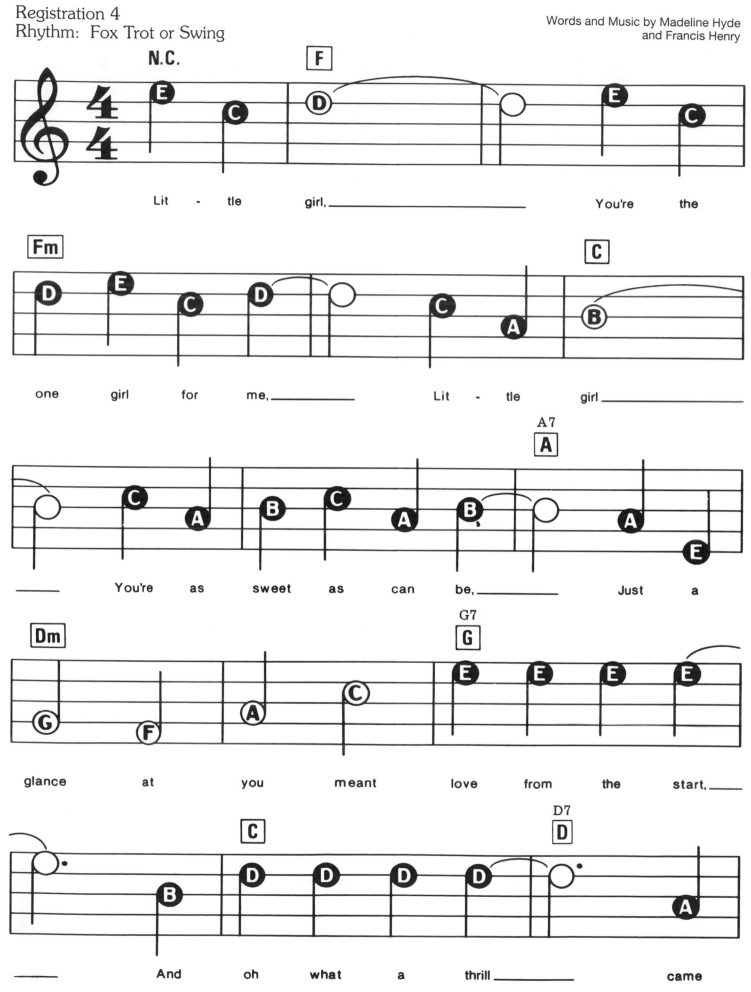

MCA Music Publishing

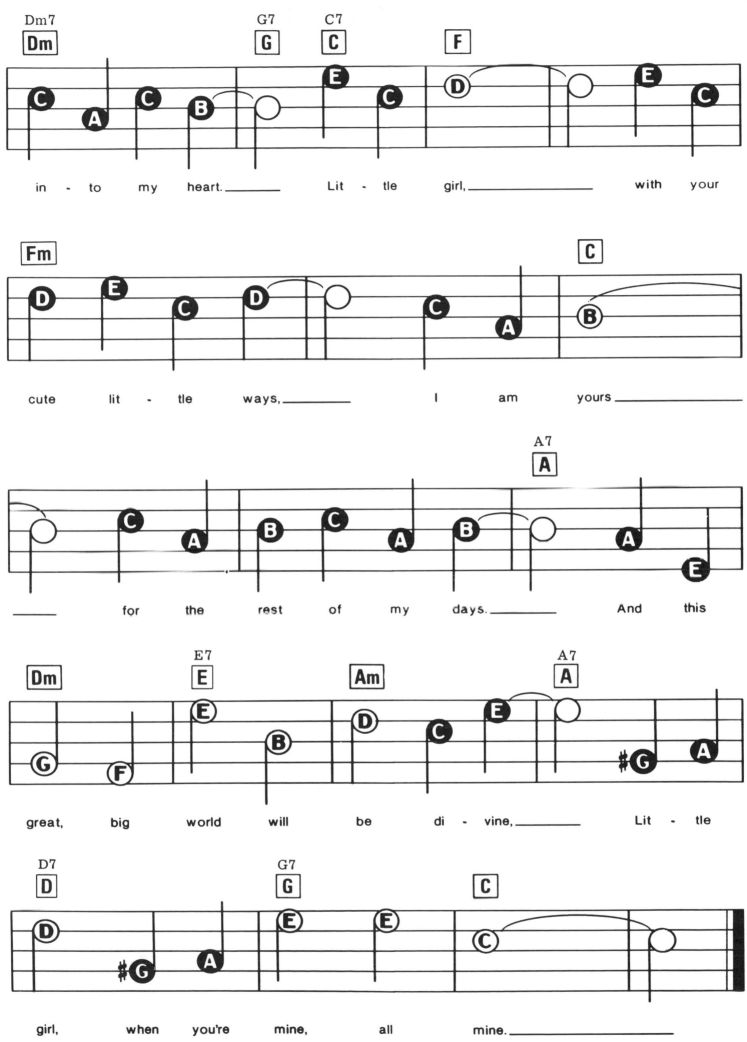

Long Ago
(And Far Away)
from COVER GIRL

Registration 3
Rhythm: Ballad or Swing

Words by Ira Gershwin
Music by Jerome Kern

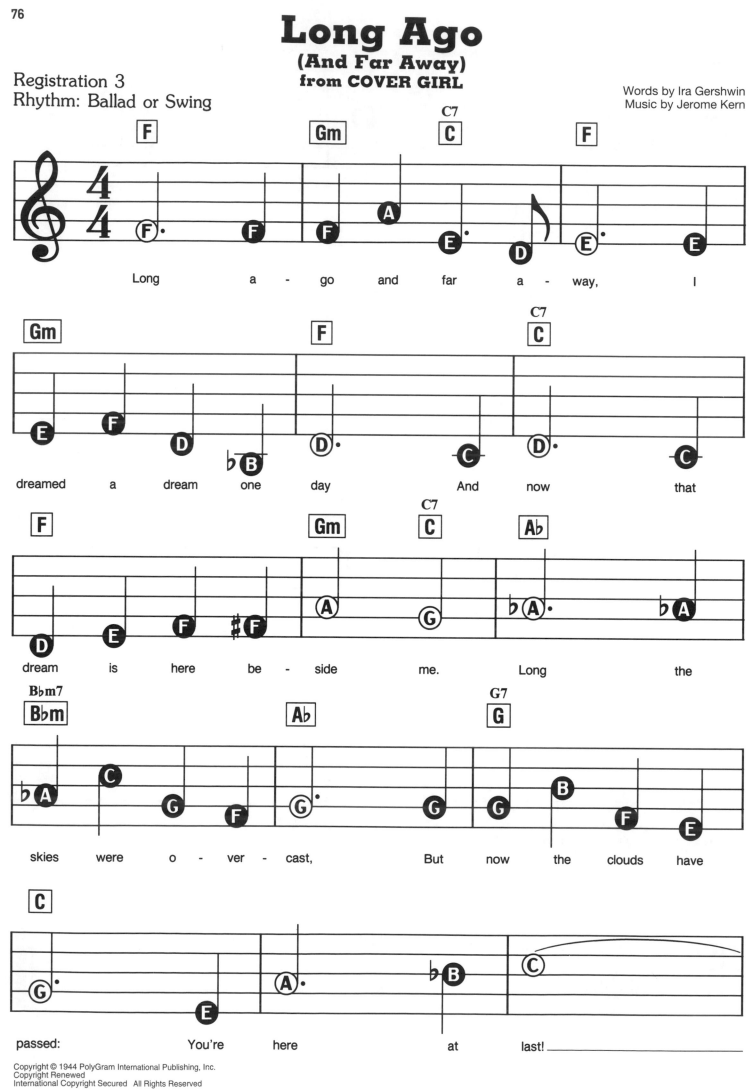

77

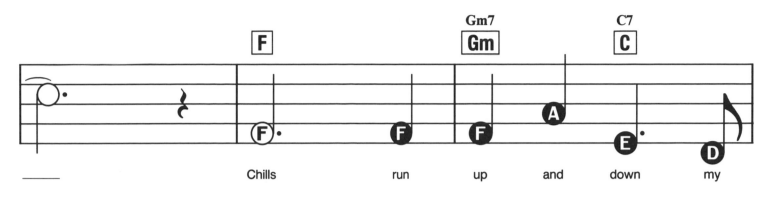

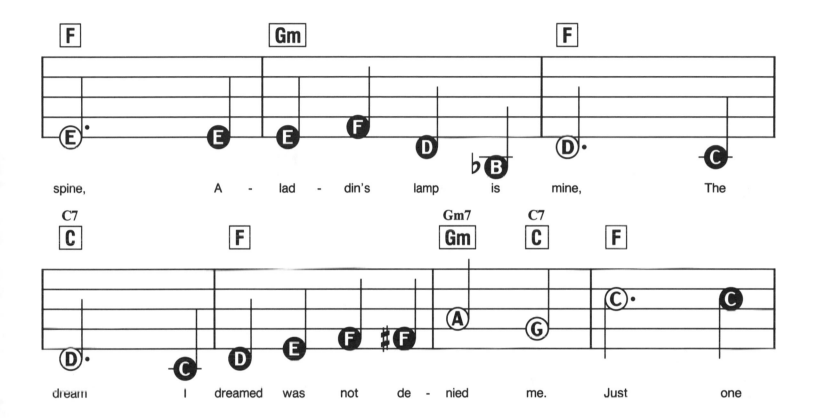

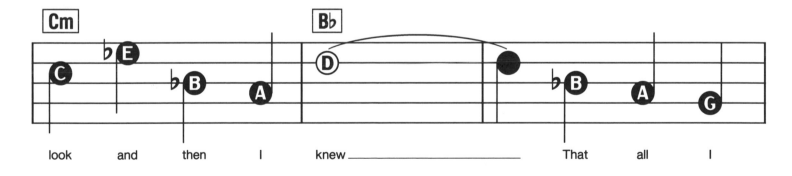

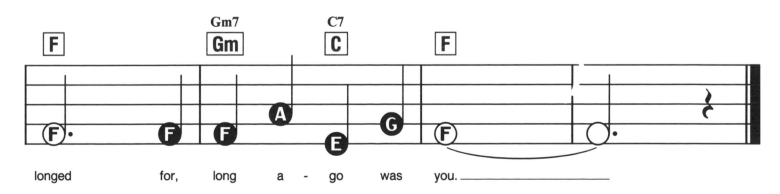

Leap Frog

Registration 8
Rhythm: Swing or Jazz

Music by
Joe Garland

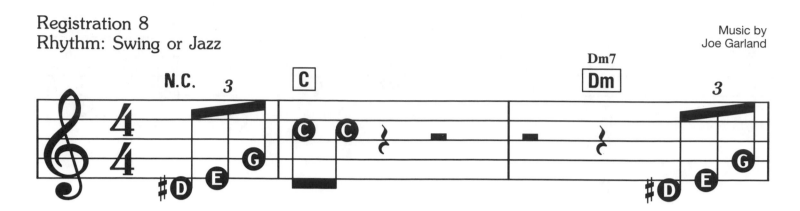

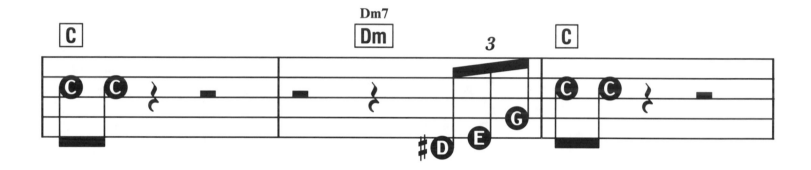

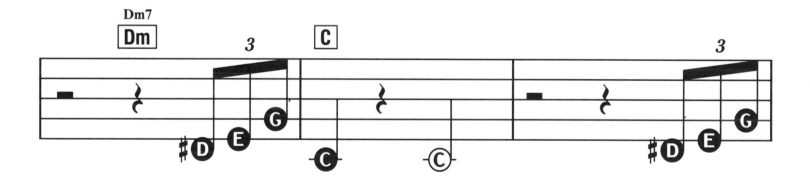

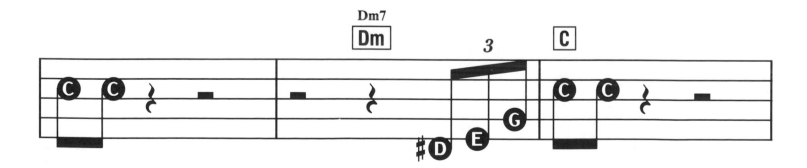

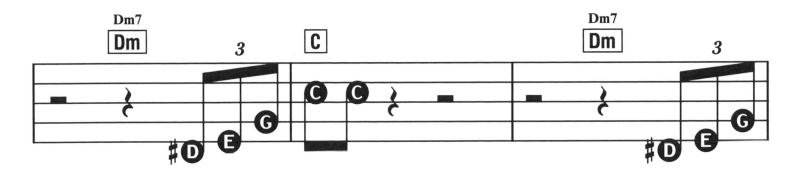

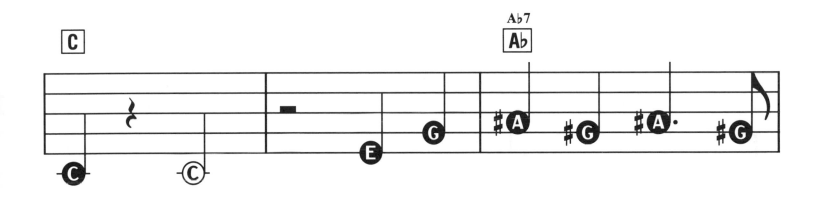

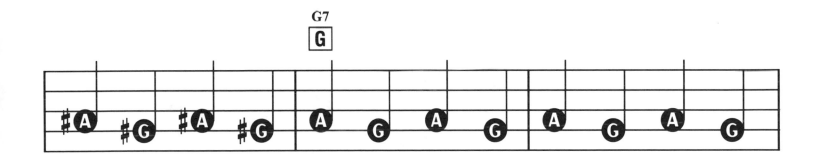

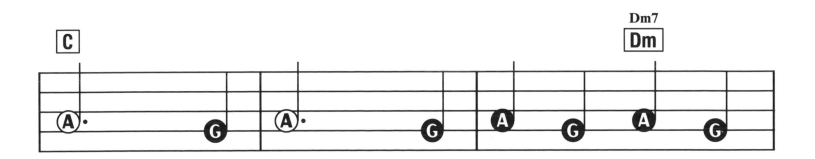

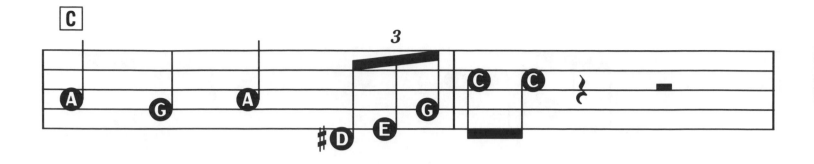

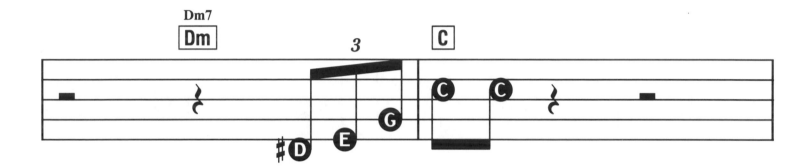

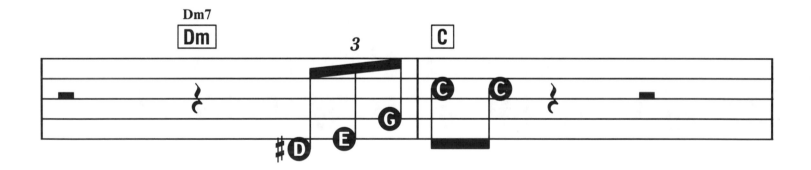

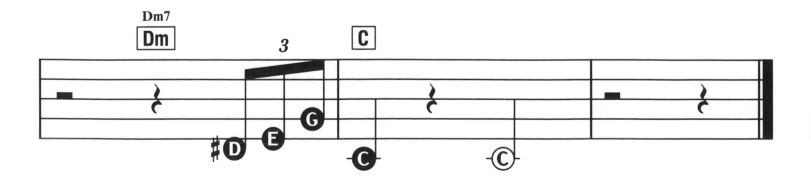

Frenesi

Registration 2
Rhythm: Rhumba or Latin

Words and Music by
Alberto Dominguez

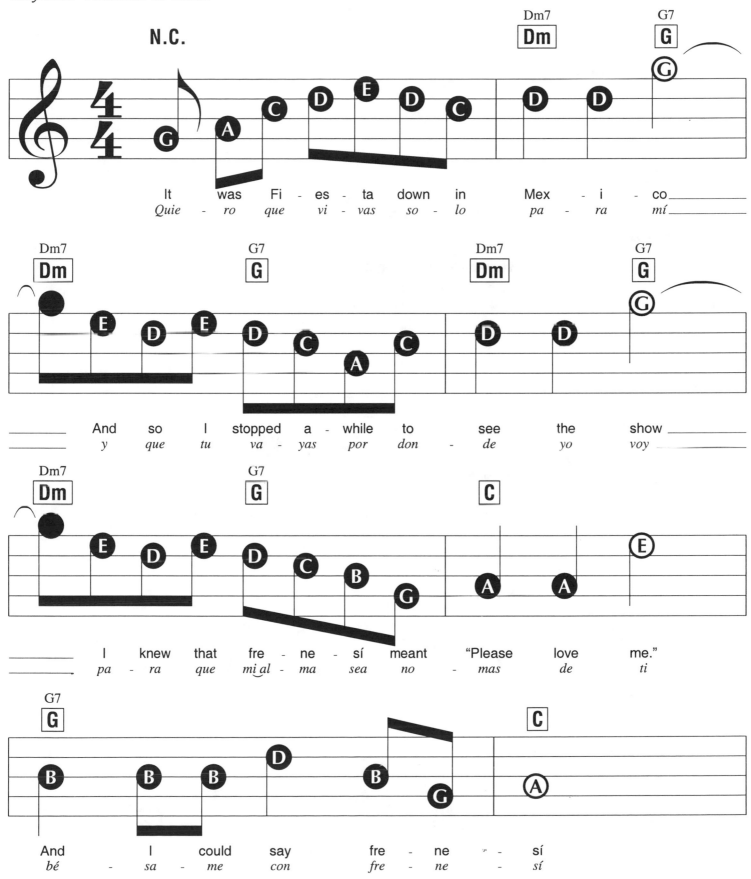

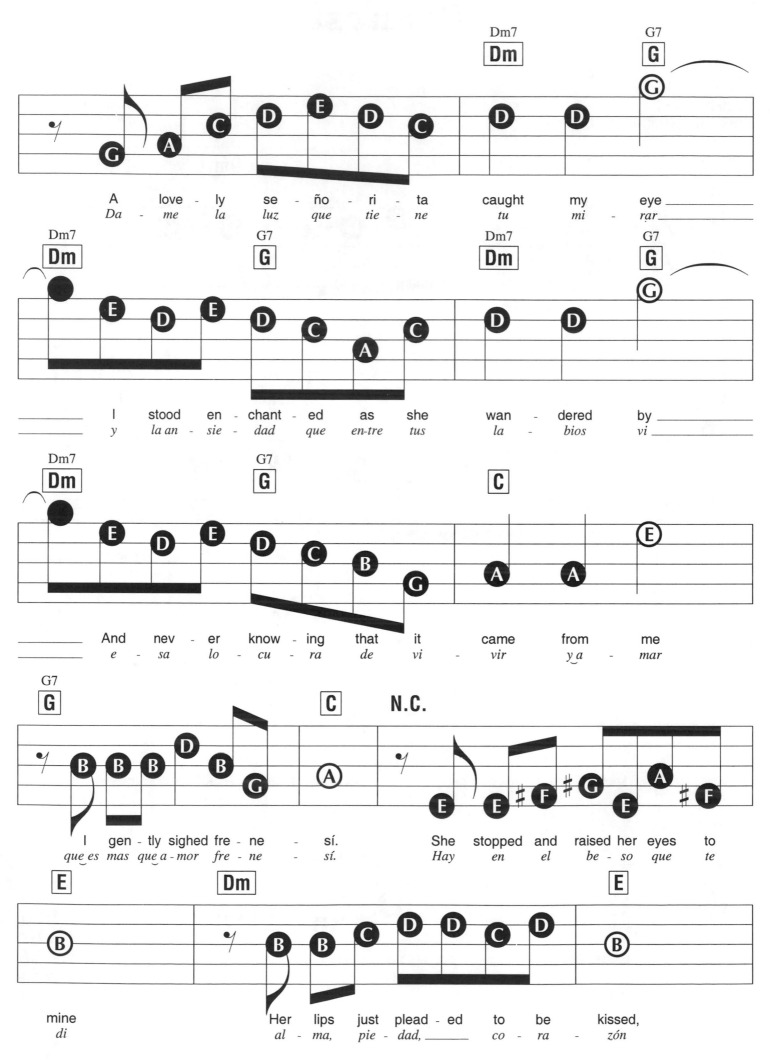

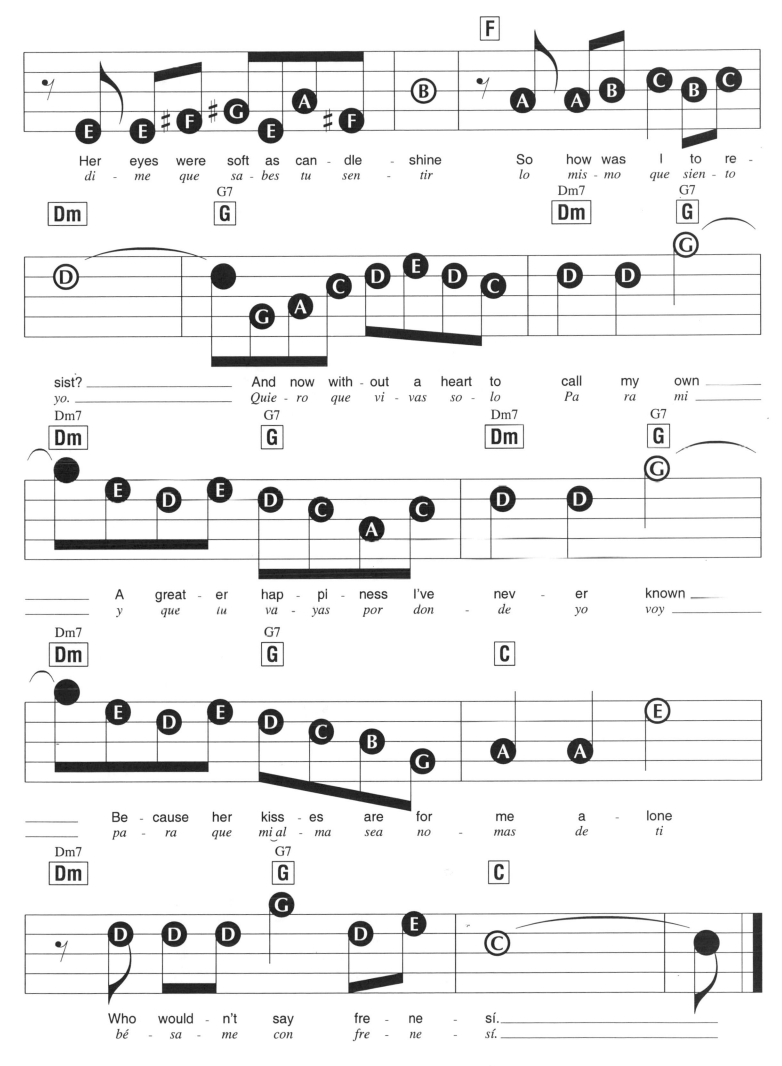

Mairzy Doats

Registration 5
Rhythm: Fox Trot or Swing

Words and Music by Milton Drake,
Al Hoffman and Jerry Livingston

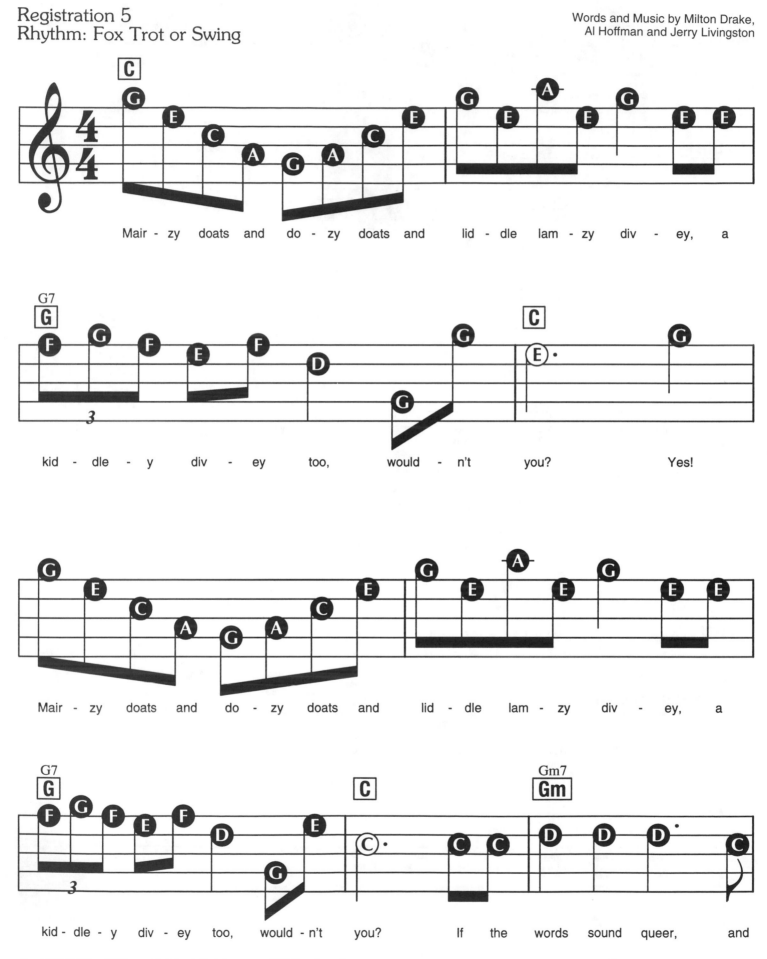

85

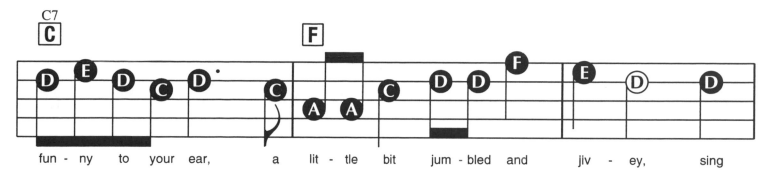

fun - ny to your ear, a lit - tle bit jum - bled and jiv - ey, sing

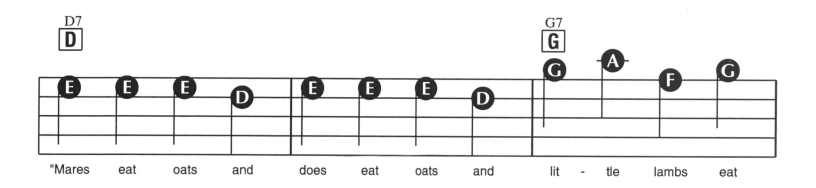

"Mares eat oats and does eat oats and lit - tle lambs eat

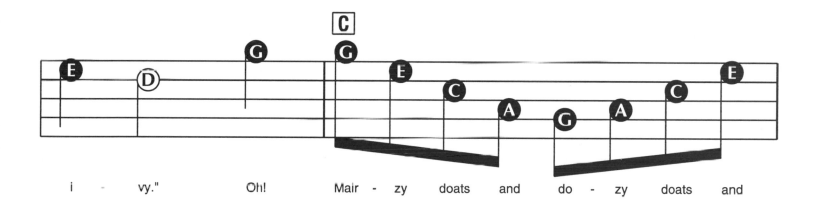

i - vy." Oh! Mair - zy doats and do - zy doats and

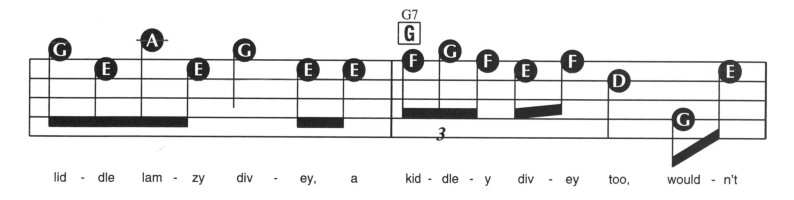

lid - dle lam - zy div - ey, a kid - dle - y div - ey too, would - n't

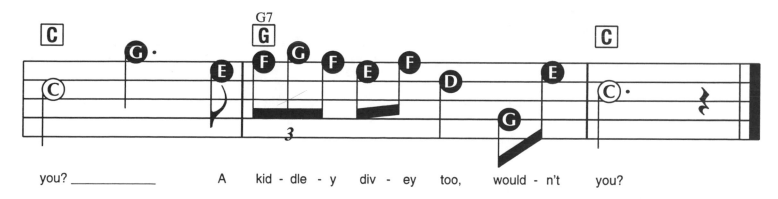

you? _____ A kid - dle - y div - ey too, would - n't you?

Marie

Registration 1
Rhythm: Fox Trot or Swing

Words and Music by
Irving Berlin

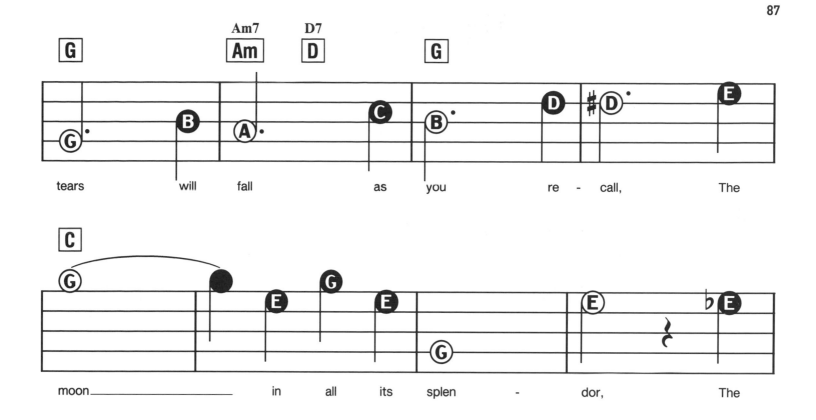

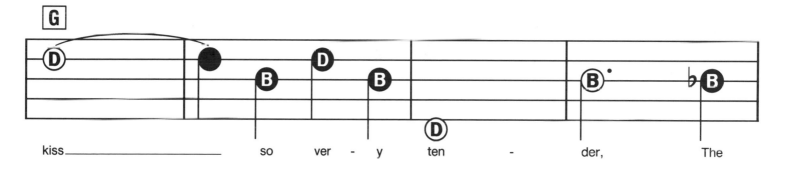

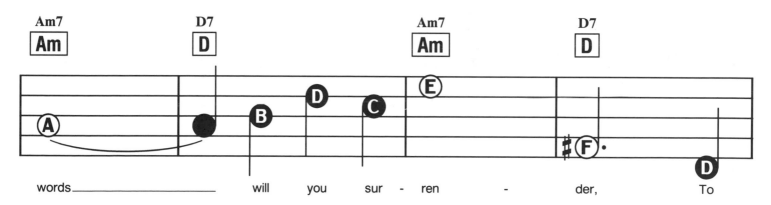

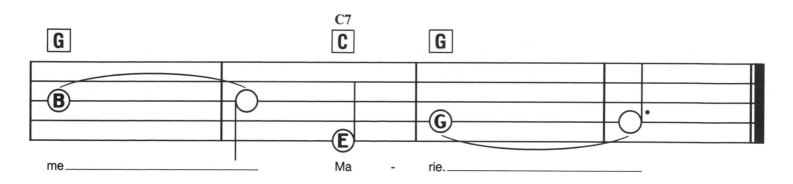

Moonglow

Registration 2
Rhythm: Fox Trot

Words and Music by Will Hudson,
Eddie DeLange and Irving Mills

My Romance
from JUMBO

Registration 5
Rhythm: Fox Trot or Ballad

Words by Lorenz Hart
Music by Richard Rodgers

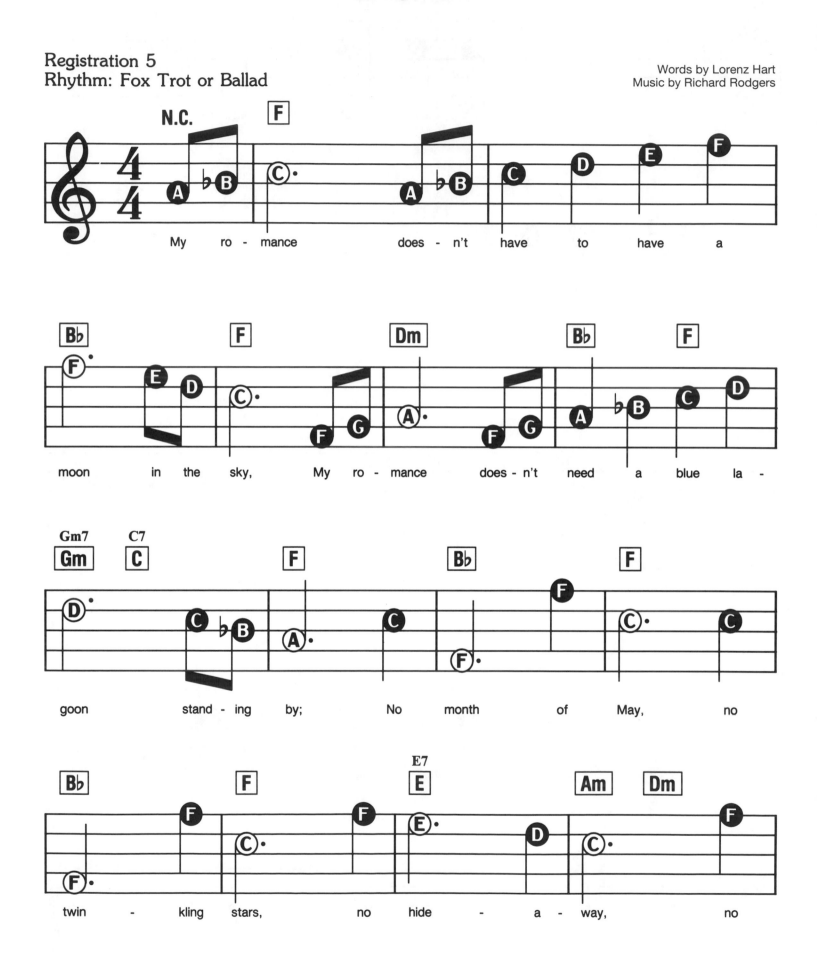

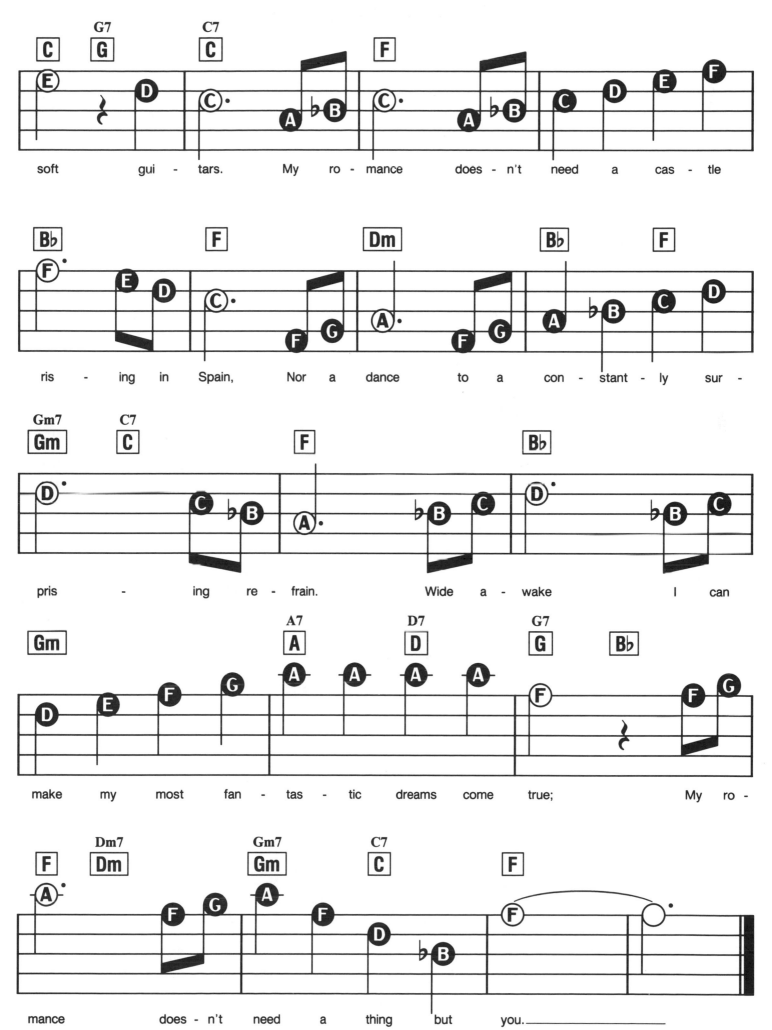

A Nightingale Sang
In Berkeley Square

Registration 2
Rhythm: Ballad

Lyric by Eric Maschwitz
Music by Manning Sherwin

93

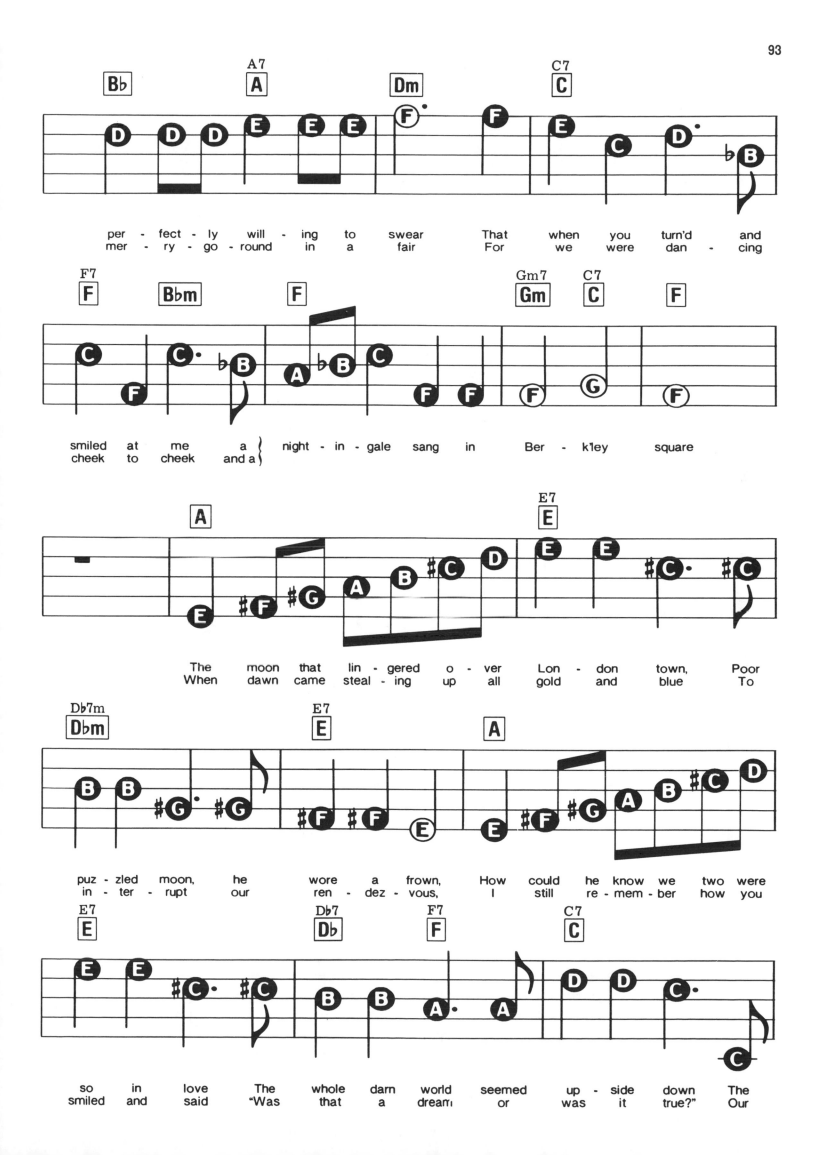

94

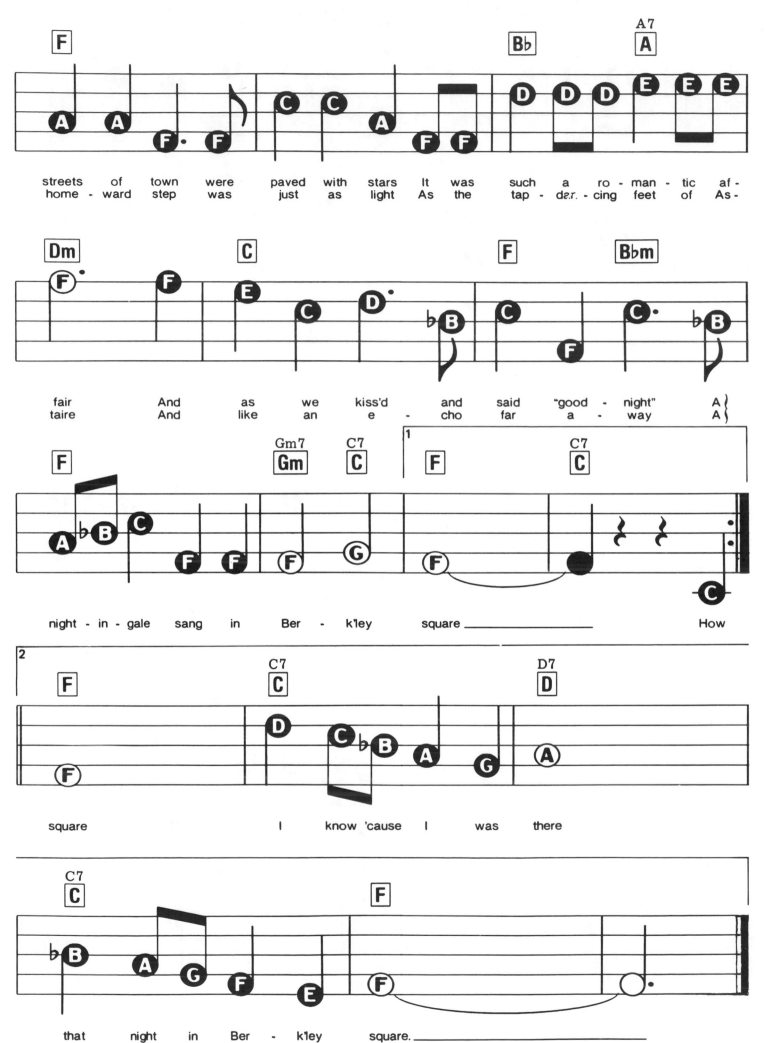

The Old Lamplighter

Registration 2
Rhythm: Swing or Jazz

Words by Charles Tobias
Music by Nat Simon

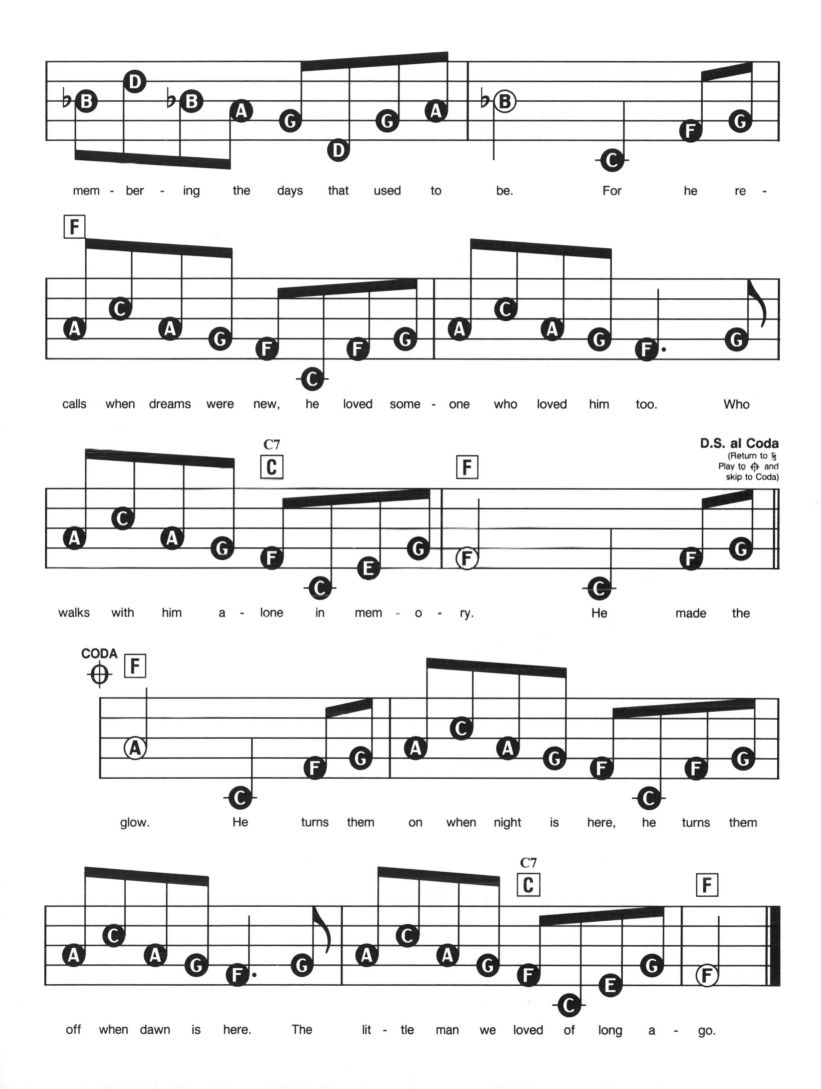

The Nearness of You
from the Paramount Picture ROMANCE IN THE DARK

Registration 9
Rhythm: Fox Trot or Swing

Words by Ned Washington
Music by Hoagy Carmichael

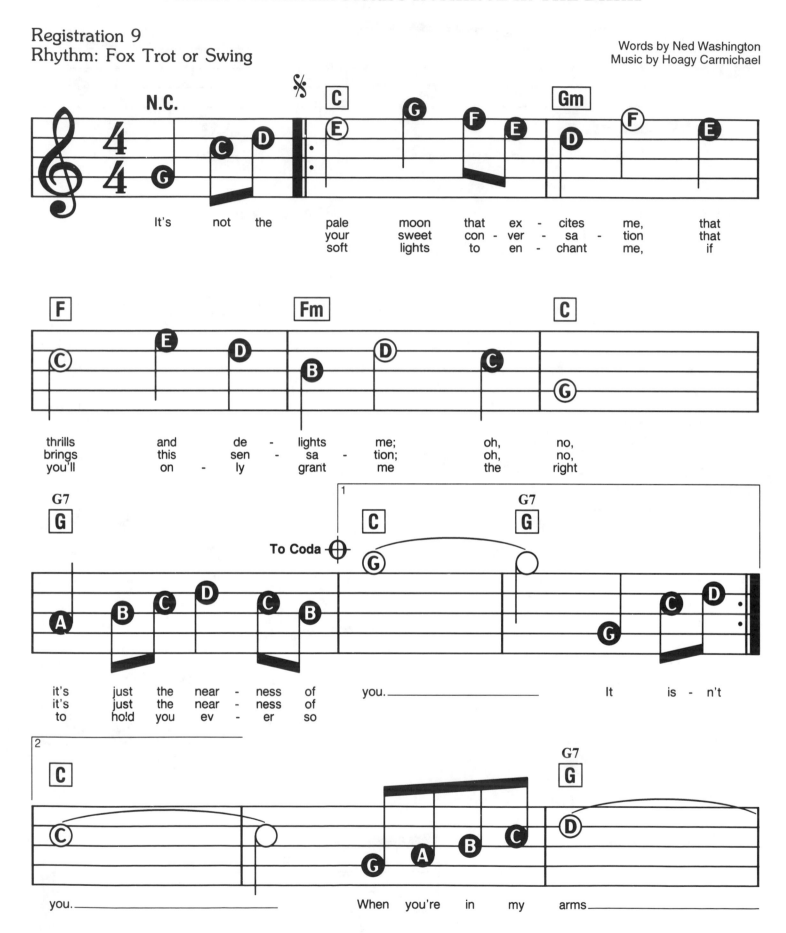

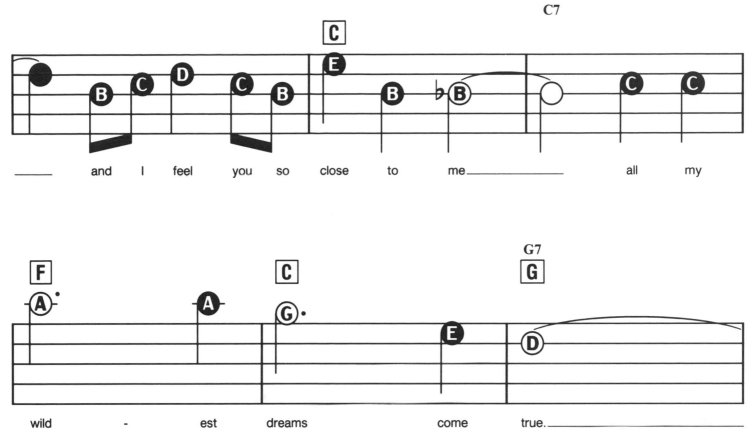

and I feel you so close to me_____ all my

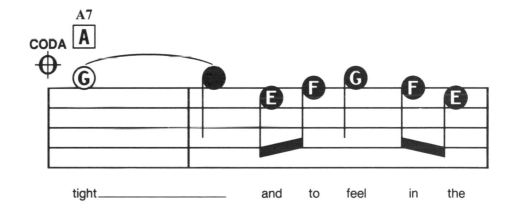

wild - est dreams come true._____

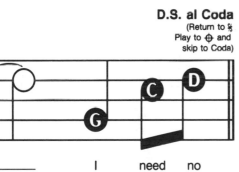

_____ I need no

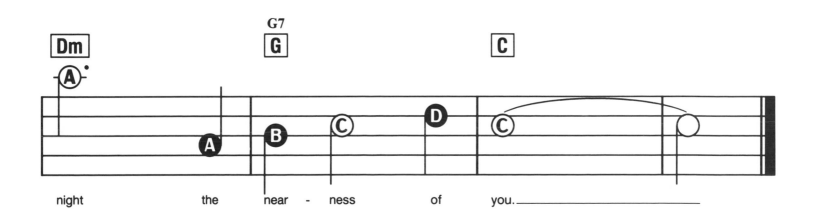

tight_____ and to feel in the

night the near - ness of you._____

On A Little Street In Singapore

Registration 1
Rhythm: Fox Trot or Swing

Words by Billy Hill
Music by Peter De Rose

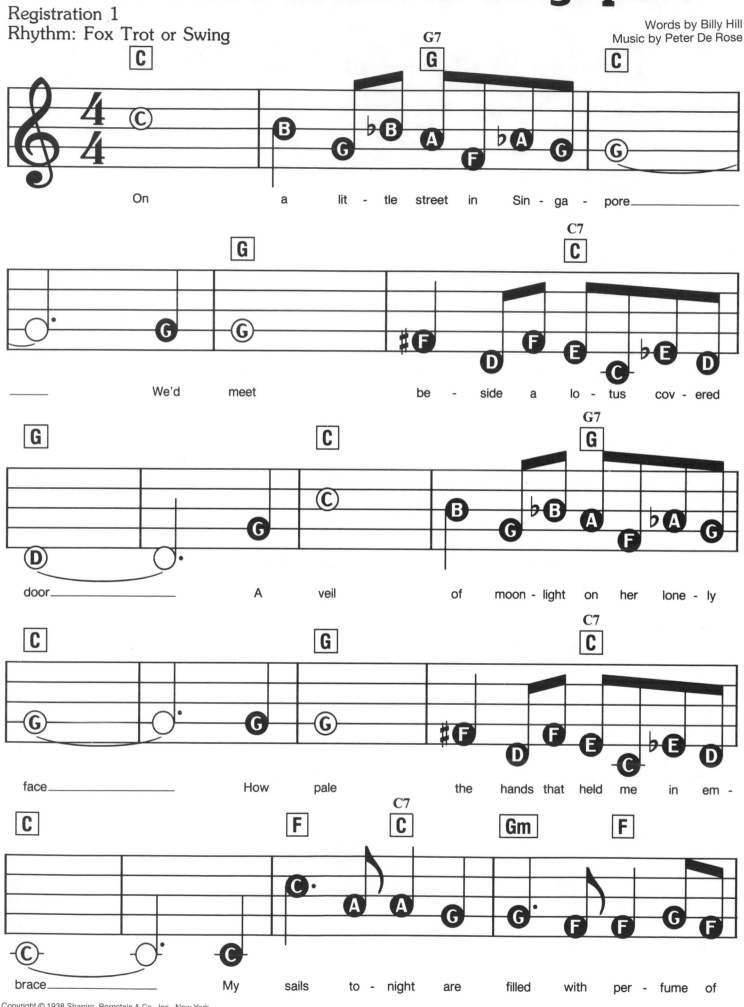

101

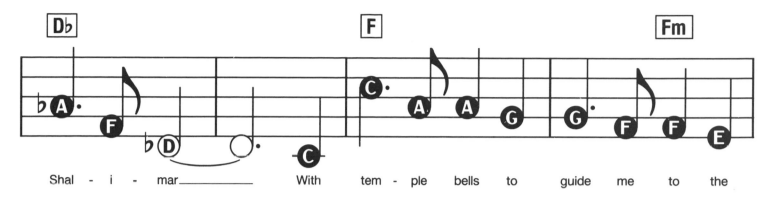

Shal - i - mar____ With tem - ple bells to guide me to the

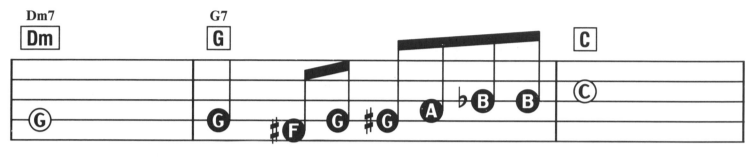

shore And then I'll hold her in my arms

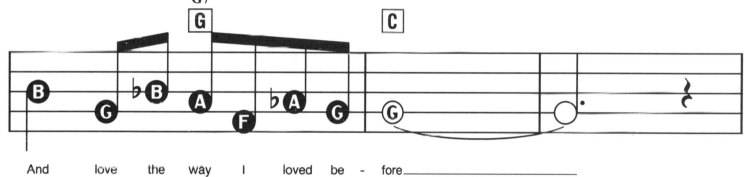

And love the way I loved be - fore____

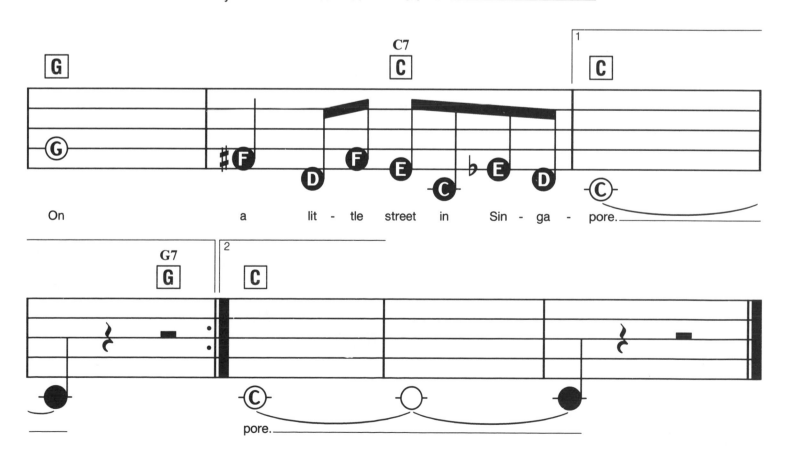

On a lit - tle street in Sin - ga - pore.____

pore.____

On The Sunny Side Of The Street

Registration 7
Rhythm: Fox Trot or Swing

Lyric by Dorothy Fields
Music by Jimmy McHugh

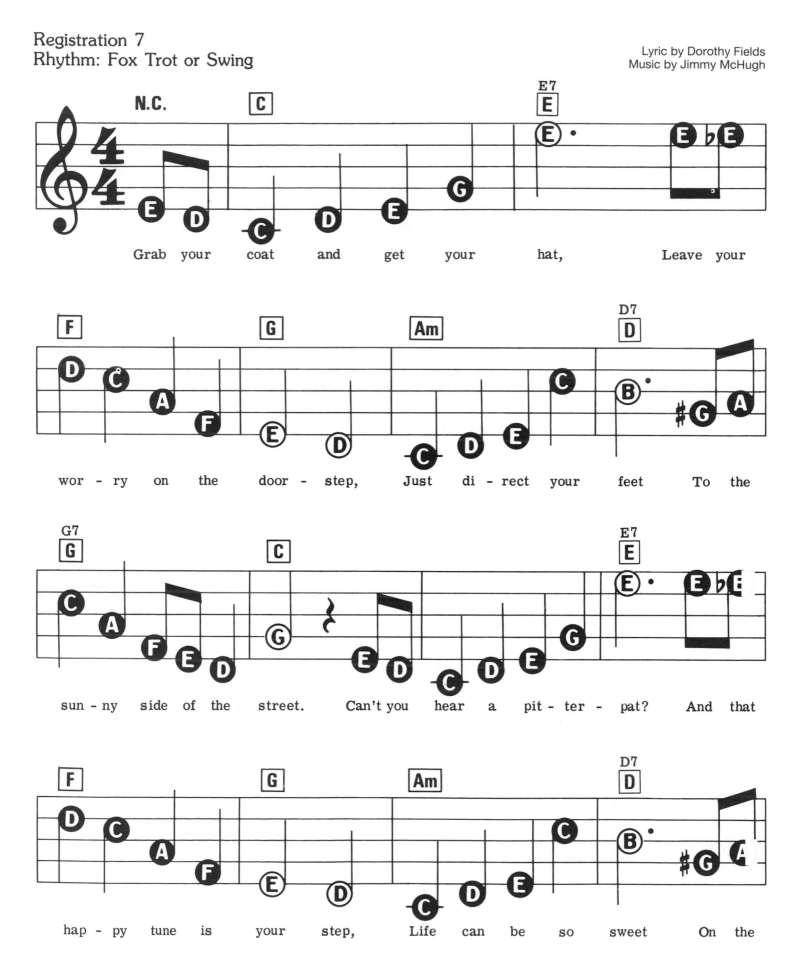

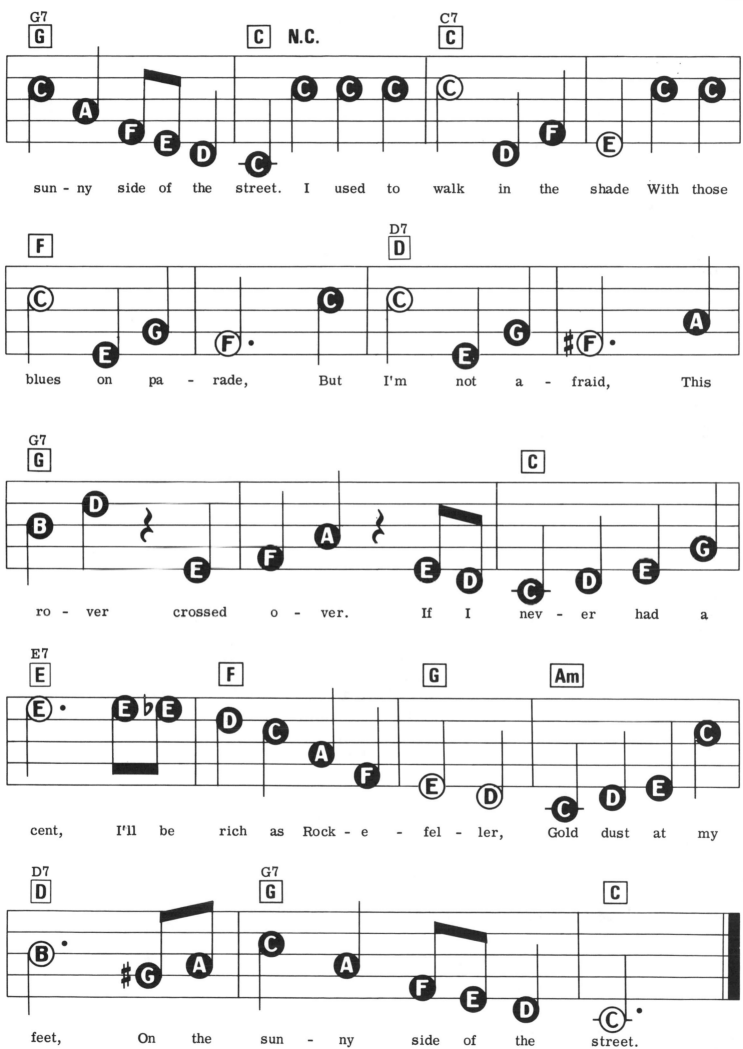

Opus One

Registration 7
Rhythm: Swing or Jazz

Words and Music by
Sy Oliver

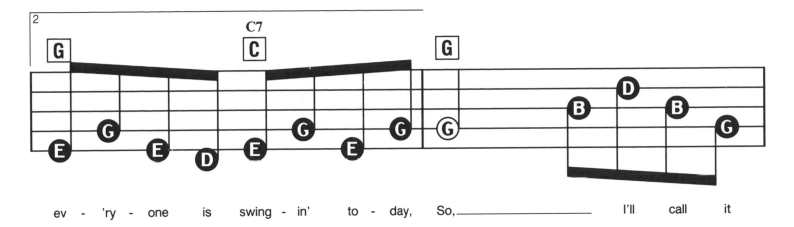

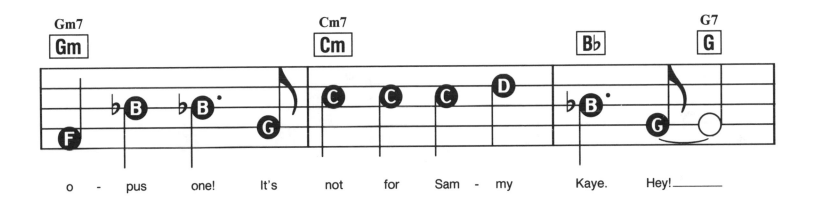

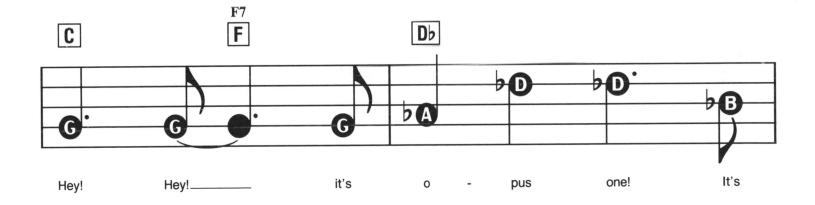

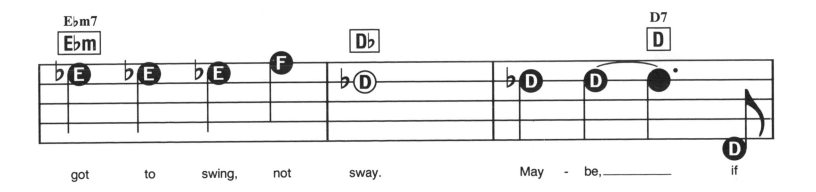

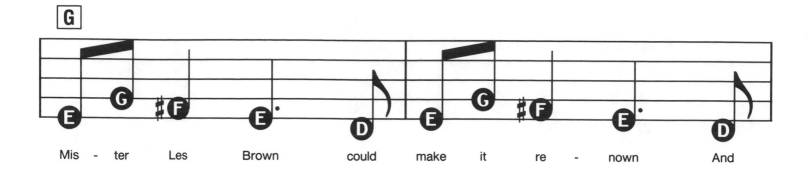

Mis - ter Les Brown could make it re - nown And

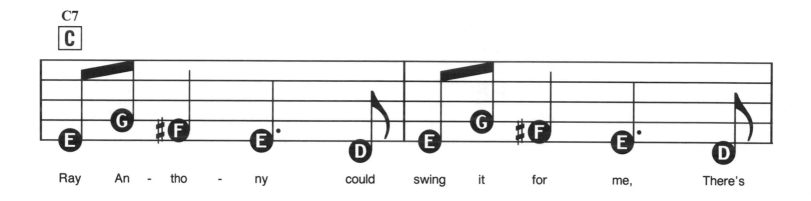

Ray An - tho - ny could swing it for me, There's

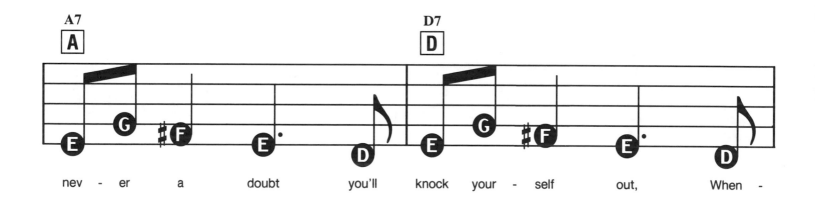

nev - er a doubt you'll knock your - self out, When -

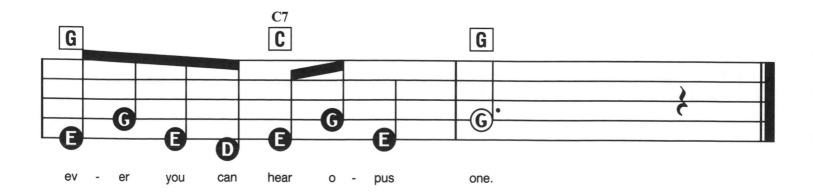

ev - er you can hear o - pus one.

Sentimental Journey

Registration 2
Rhythm: Fox Trot or Swing

Words and Music by Bud Green,
Les Brown and Ben Homer

108

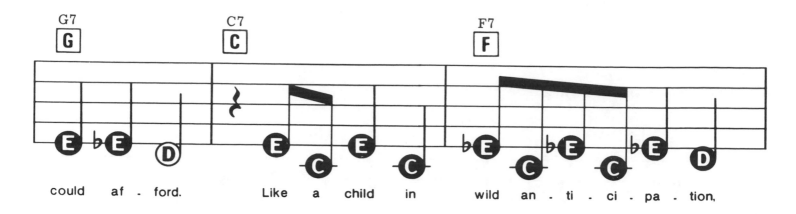

could af - ford.   Like   a   child   in   wild an - ti - ci - pa - tion,

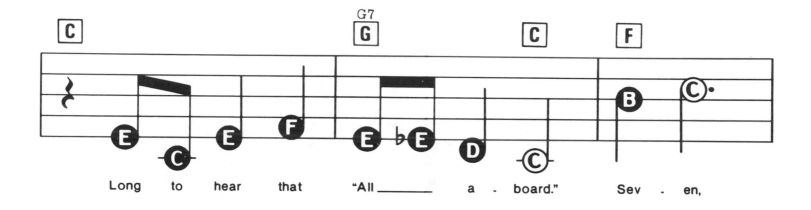

Long   to   hear   that   "All _____ a - board."   Sev - en,

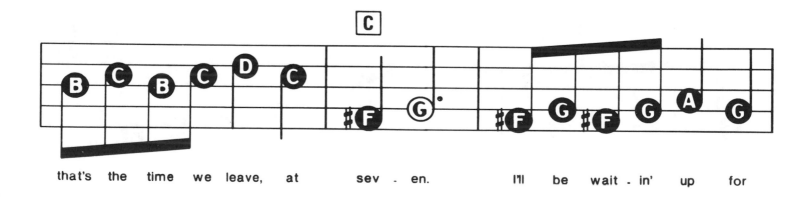

that's the time we leave,   at   sev - en.   I'll be wait - in' up for

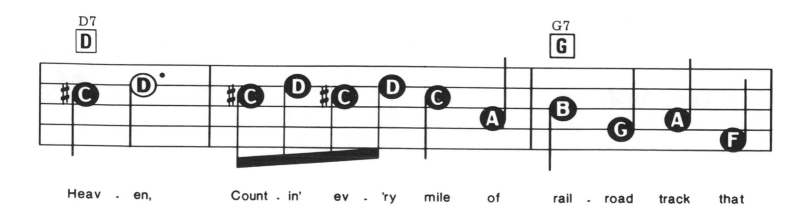

Heav - en,   Count - in' ev - 'ry mile of   rail - road track that

109

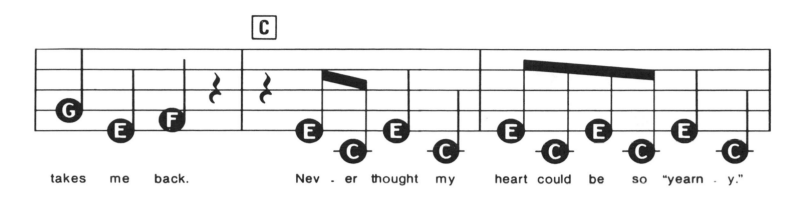

takes me back. Nev - er thought my heart could be so "yearn - y."

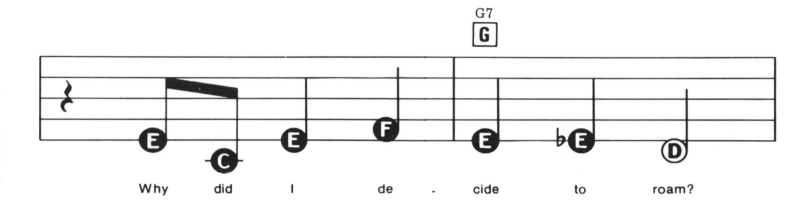

Why did I de - cide to roam?

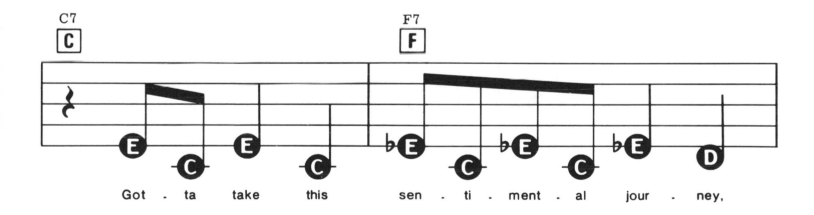

Got - ta take this sen - ti - ment - al jour - ney,

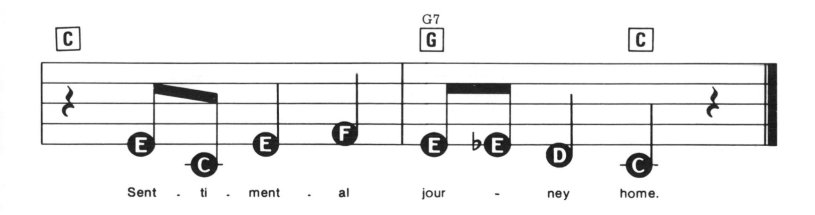

Sent - i - ment - al jour - ney home.

Satin Doll

Registration 4
Rhythm: Swing or Jazz

Words by Johnny Mercer
Music by Billy Strayhorn and Duke Ellington

111

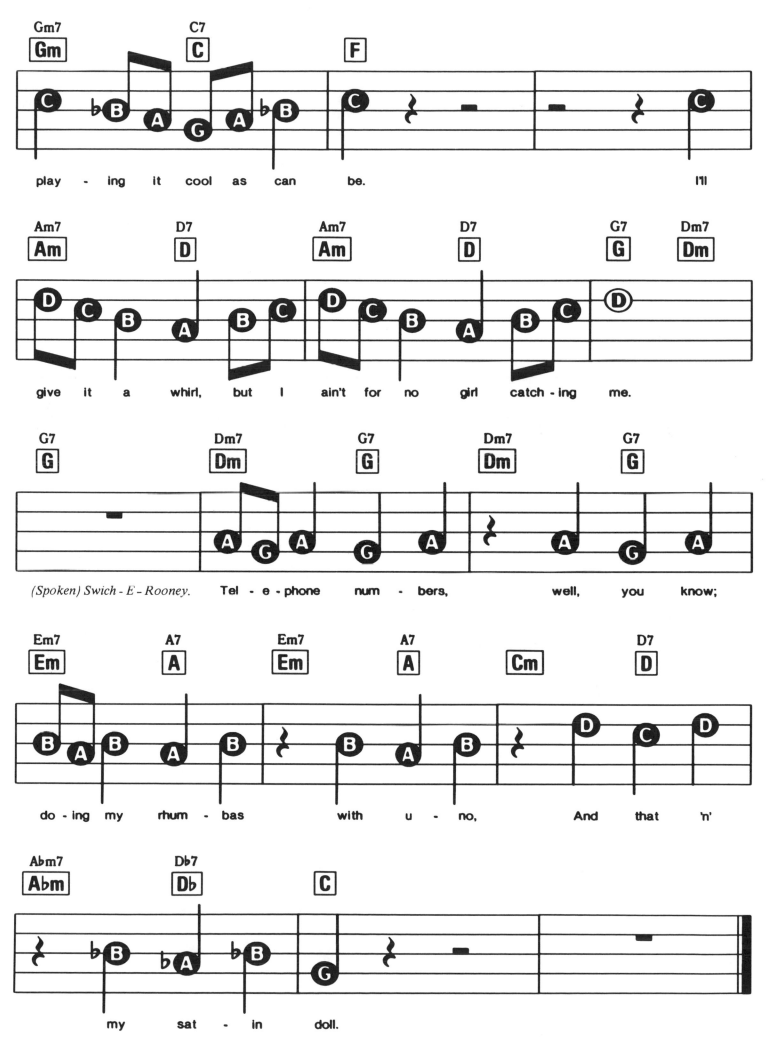

Penthouse Serenade

Registration 1
Rhythm: Swing

Words and Music by Will Jason
and Val Burton

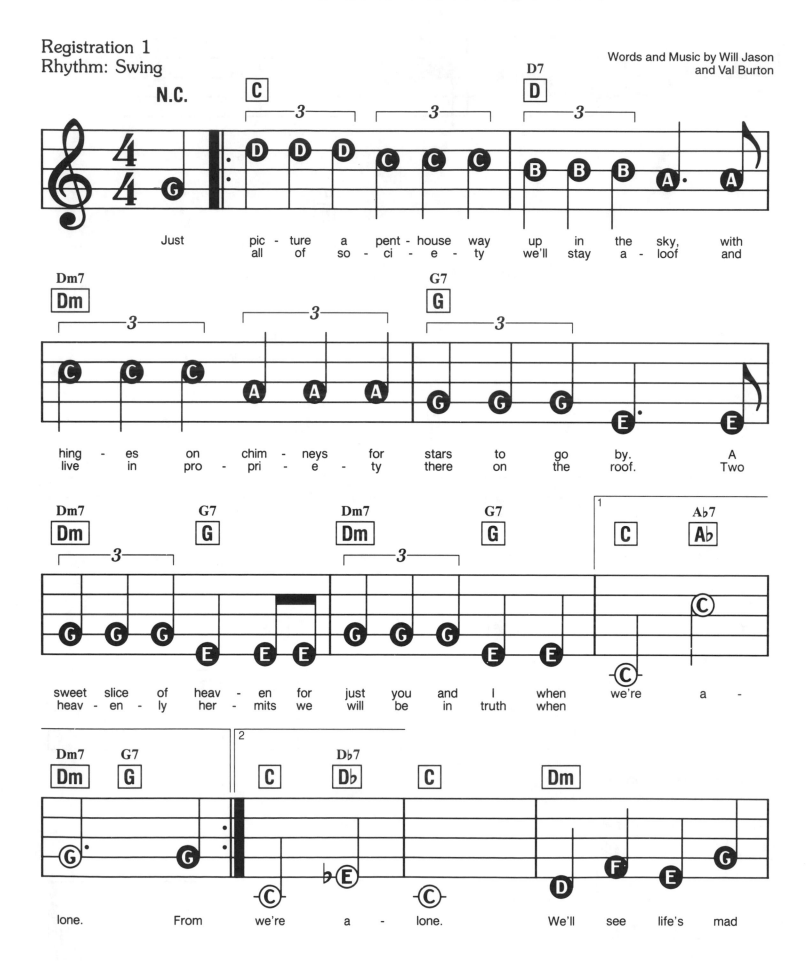

113

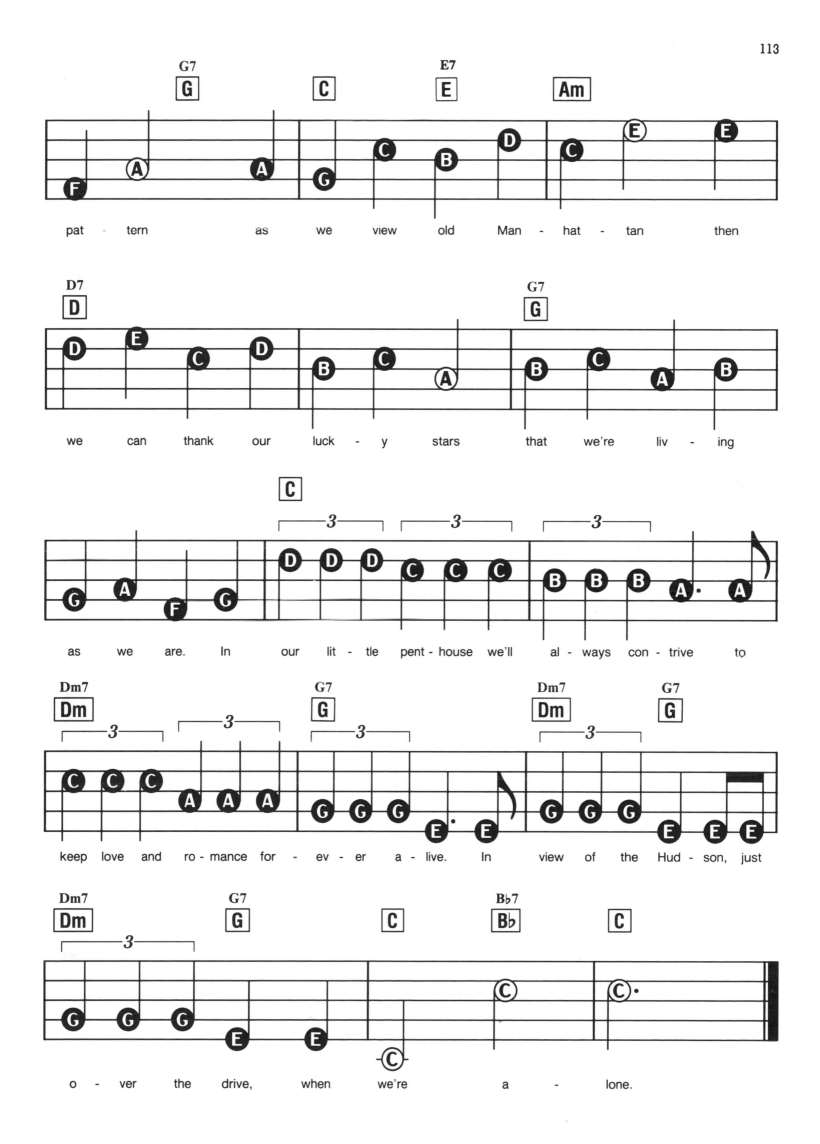

Seems Like Old Times

Registration 5
Rhythm: Swing or Jazz

Words and Music by John Jacob Loeb
and Carmen Lombardo

115

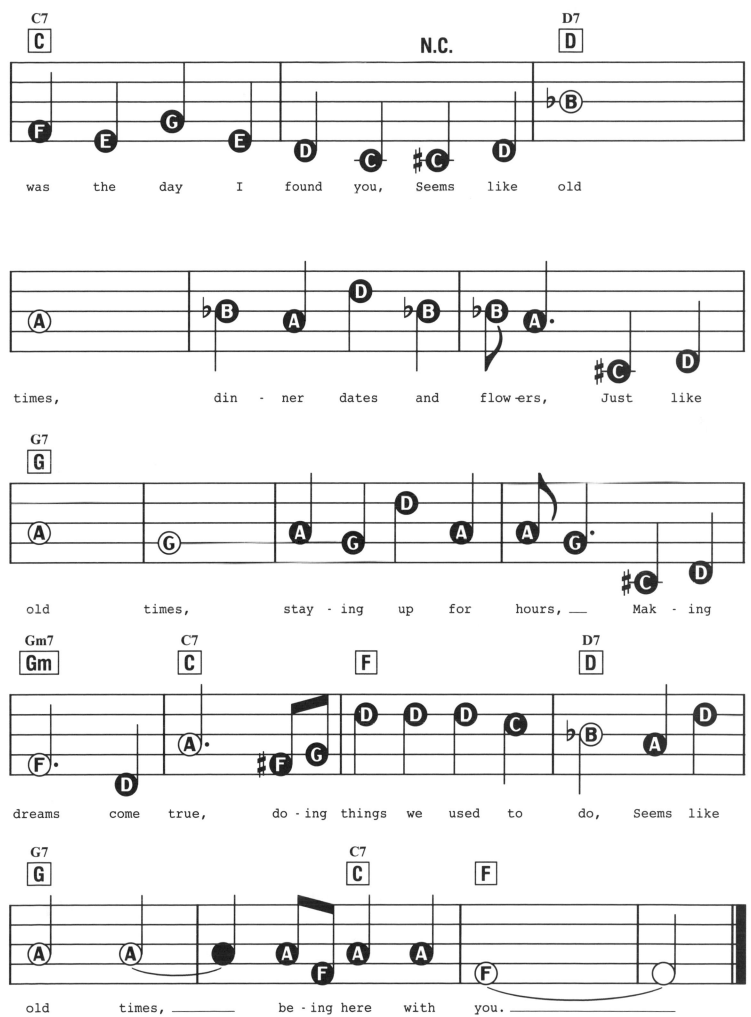

Tangerine
from the Paramount Picture THE FLEET'S IN

Registration 9
Rhythm: Swing

Words by Johnny Mercer
Music by Victor Schertzinger

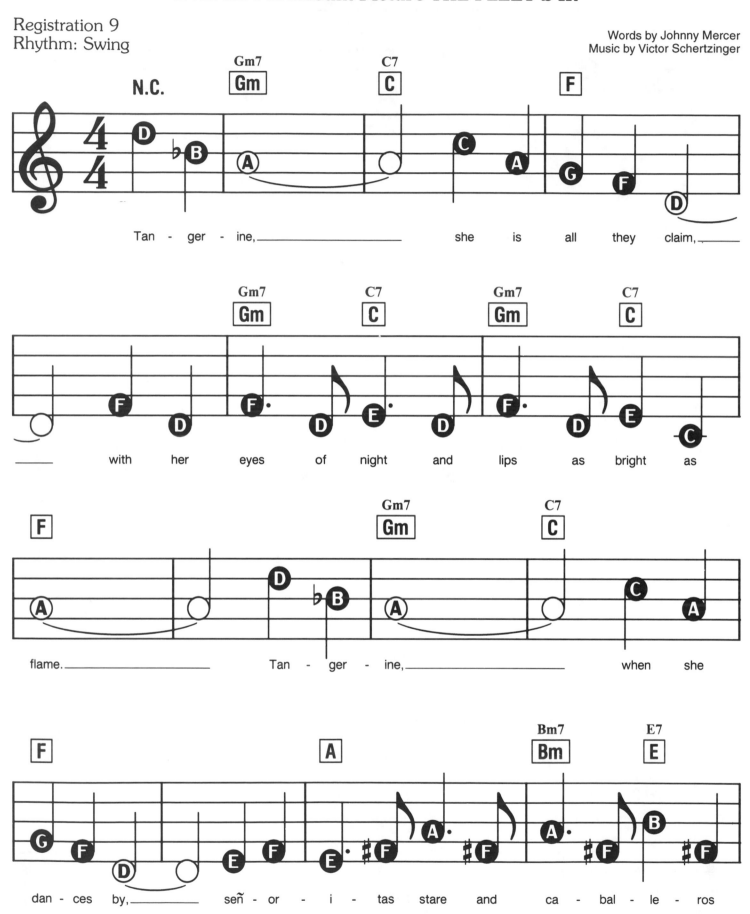

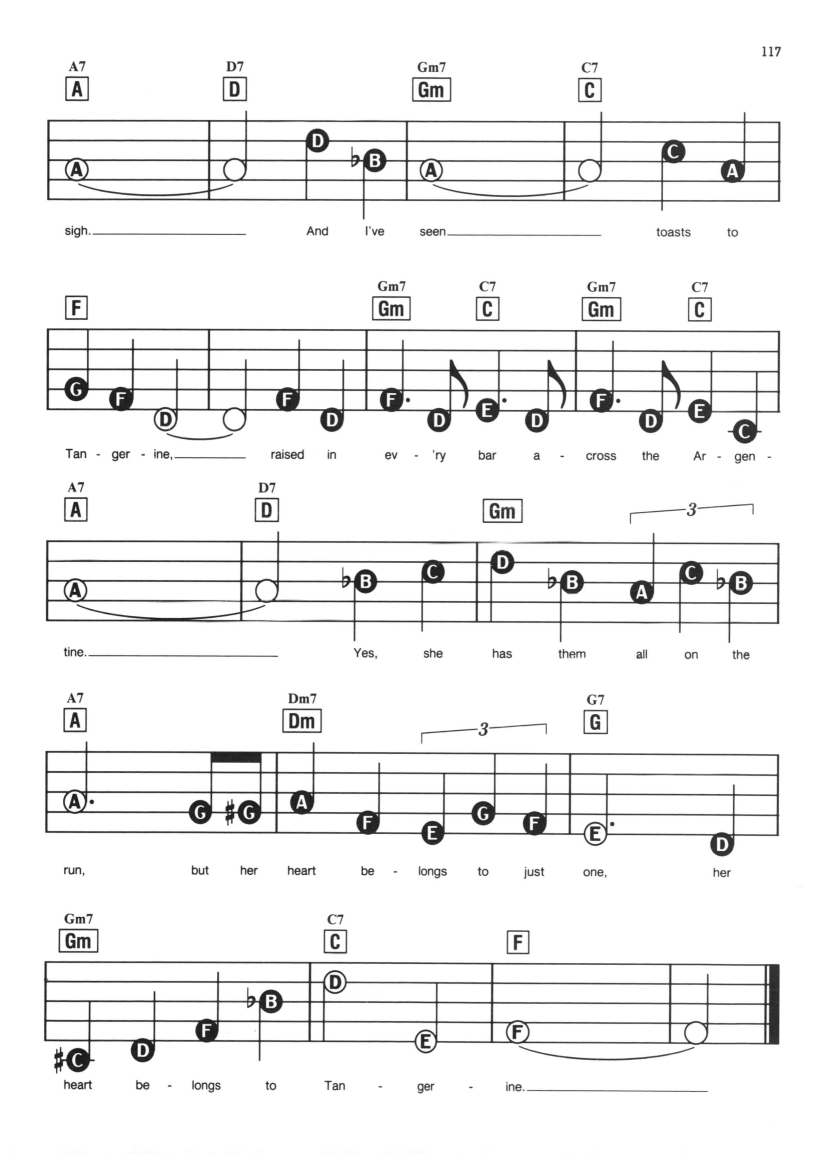

Somebody Else Is Taking
My Place

Registration 8
Rhythm: Fox Trot or Swing

Words and Music by Dick Howard,
Bob Ellsworth and Russ Morgan

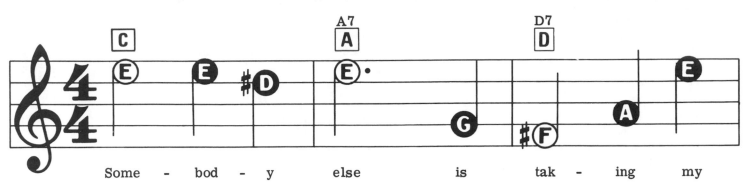

Some - bod - y   else   is   tak - ing   my

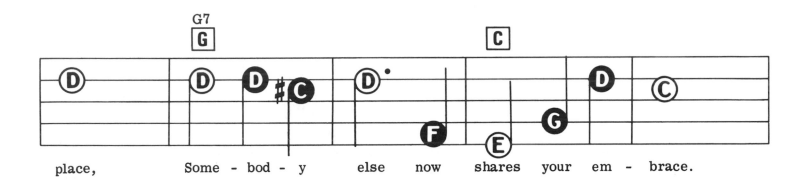

place,   Some - bod - y   else   now   shares   your   em - brace.

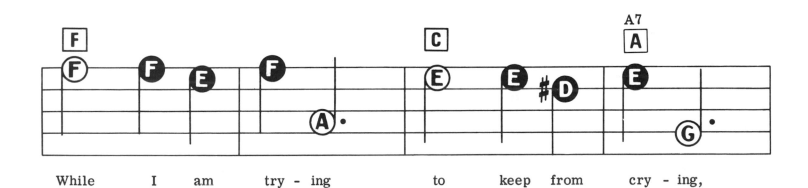

While   I   am   try - ing   to   keep   from   cry - ing,

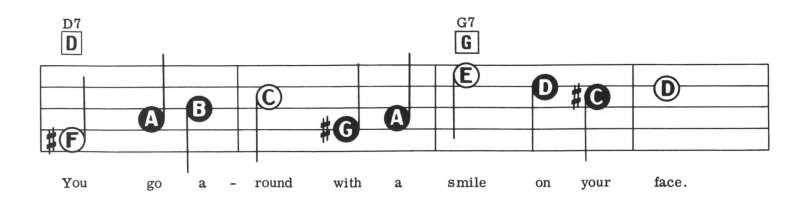

You   go   a - round   with   a   smile   on   your   face.

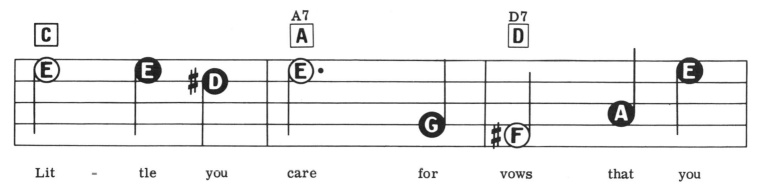

Lit - tle you care for vows that you

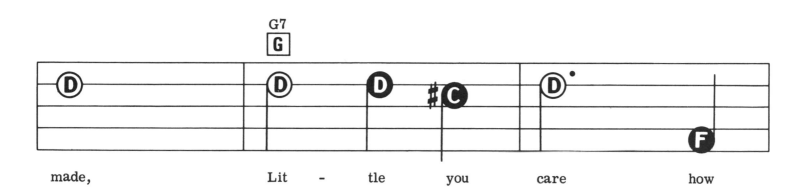

made, Lit - tle you care how

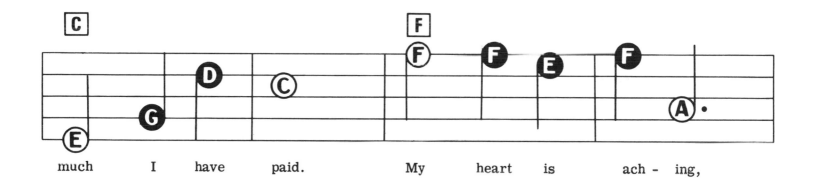

much I have paid. My heart is ach - ing,

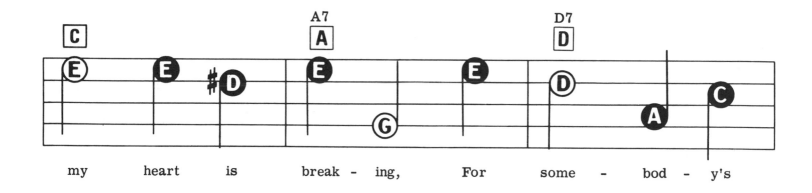

my heart is break - ing, For some - bod - y's

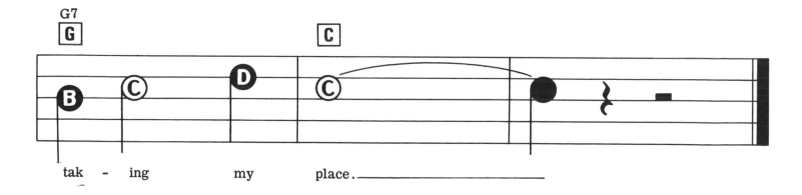

tak - ing my place.

Somebody Loves You

Registration 8
Rhythm: Fox Trot or Swing

Words by Charlie Tobias
Music by Peter De Rose

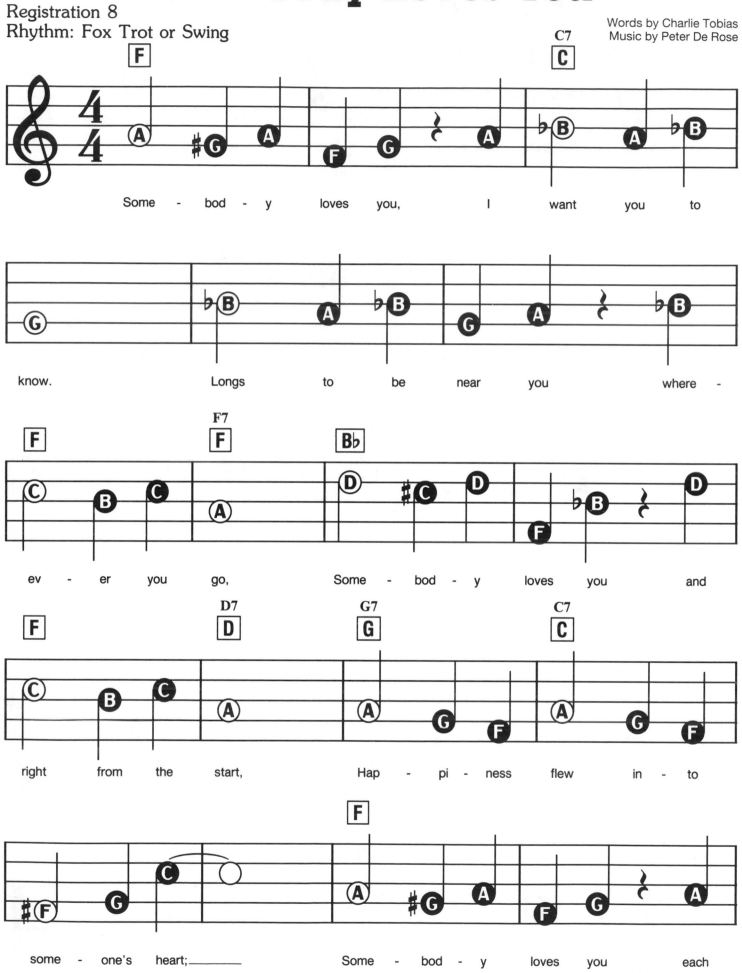

121

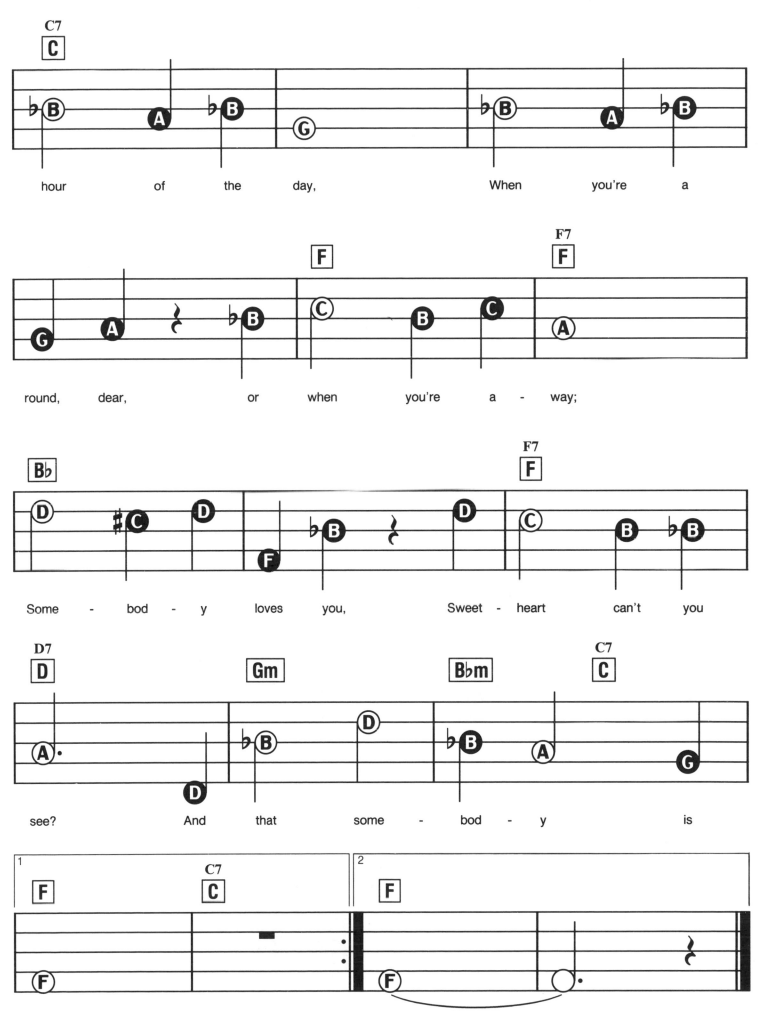

Sometimes I'm Happy

Registration 2
Rhythm: Swing

Words by Clifford Grey and Irving Caesar
Music by Vincent Youmans

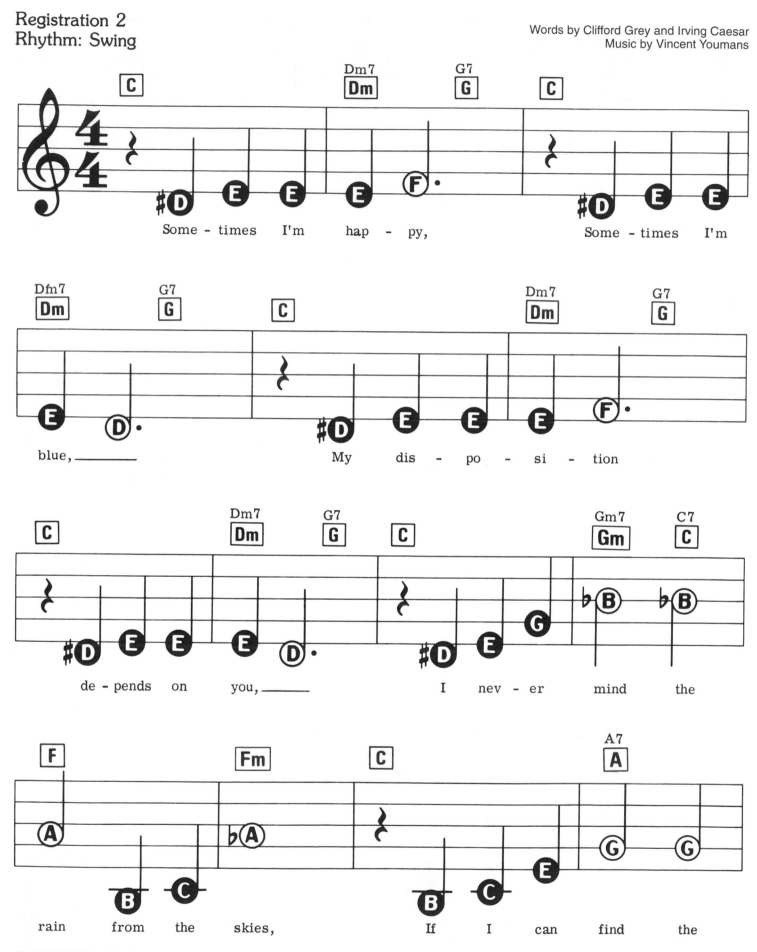

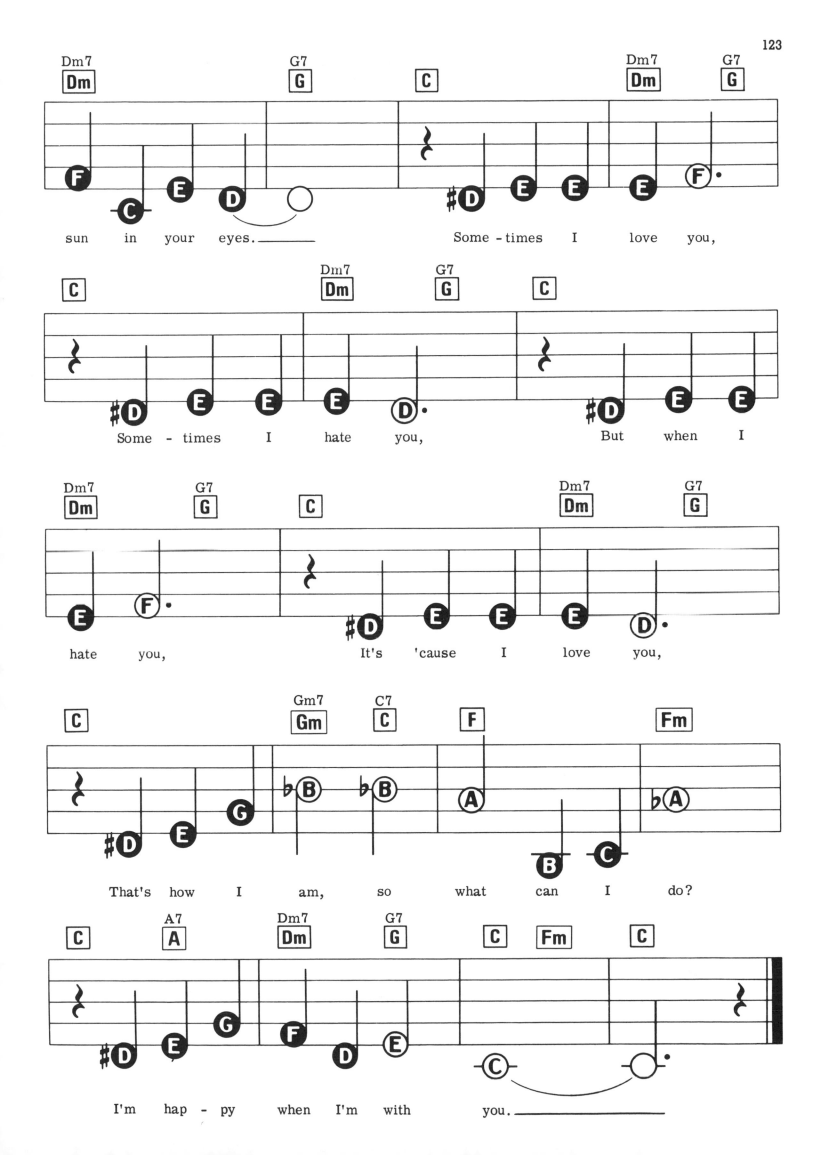

A String of Pearls
from THE GLENN MILLER STORY

Registration 4
Rhythm: Swing

Words by Eddie DeLange
Music by Jerry Gray

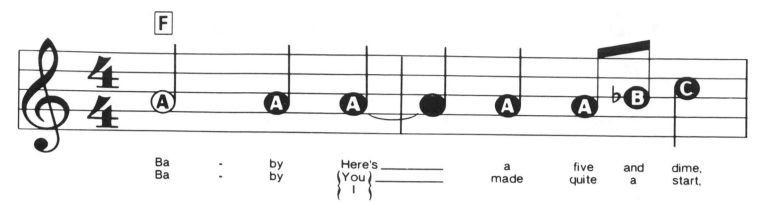

Ba - by Here's _____ a five and dime,
Ba - by (You) (I) _____ a made quite a start,

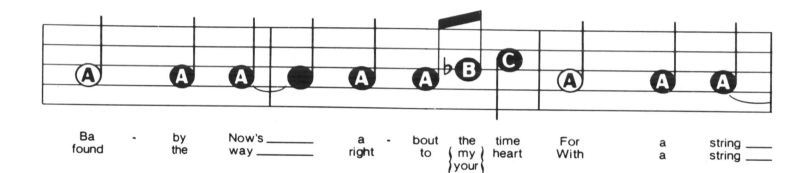

Ba - by Now's _____ a - bout the time For a string _____
found by the way _____ right to (my) (your) heart With a string _____

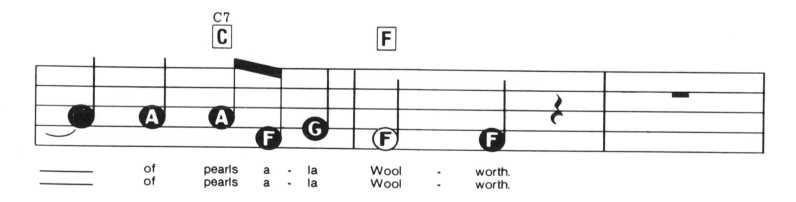

_____ of pearls a - la Wool - worth.
_____ of pearls a - la Wool - worth.

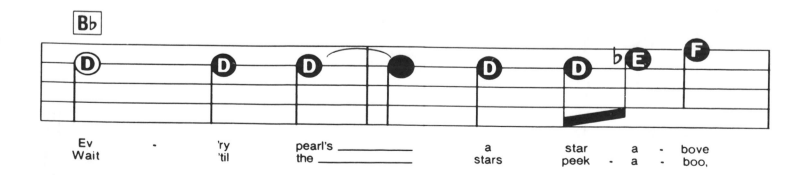

Ev - 'ry pearl's _____ a star a - bove
Wait 'til the _____ stars peek - a - boo,

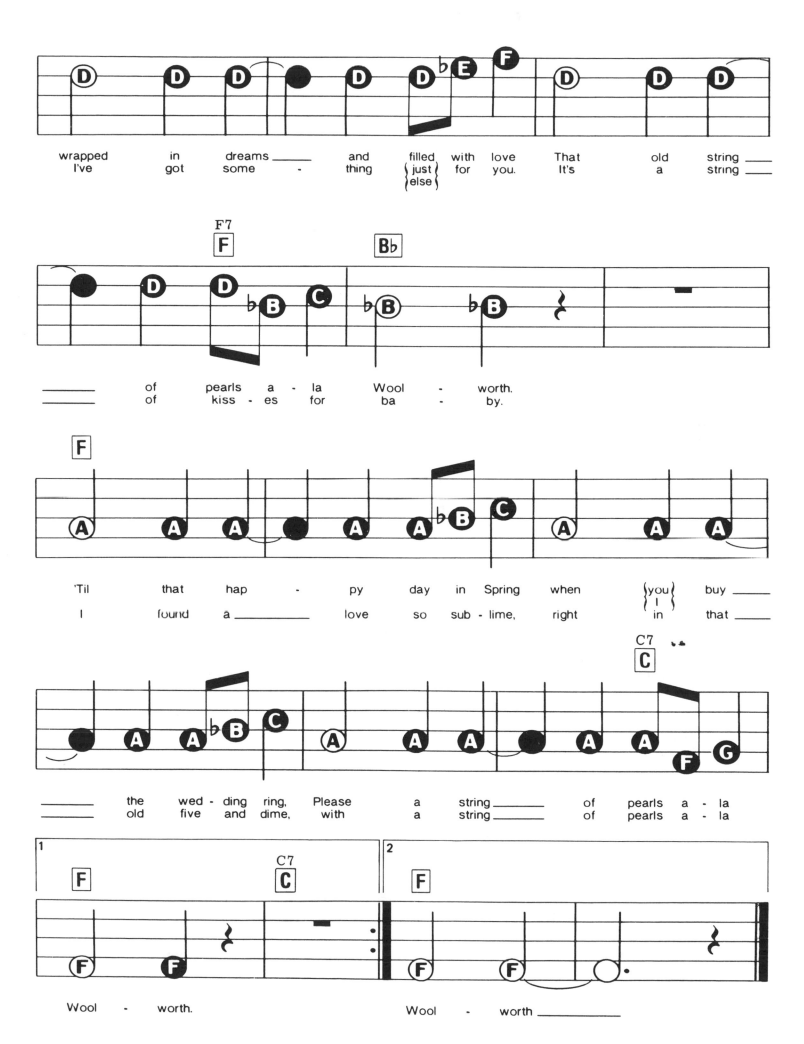

Sunrise Serenade

Registration 9
Rhythm: Fox Trot or Swing

Words by Jack Lawrence
Music by Frankie Carle

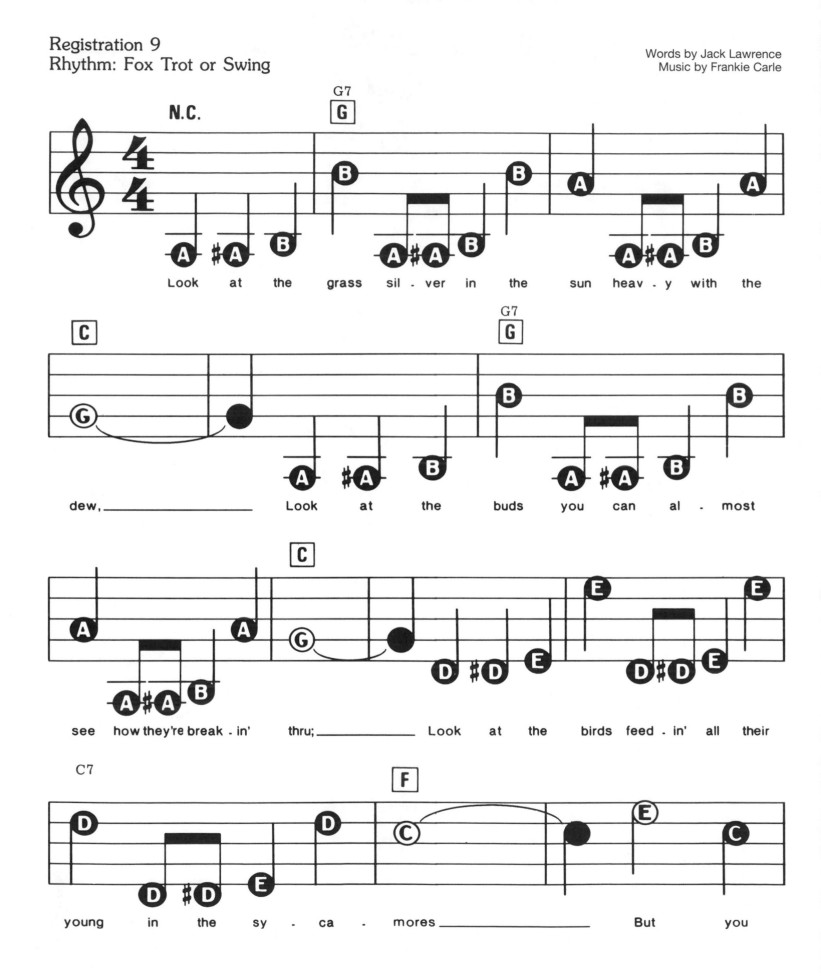

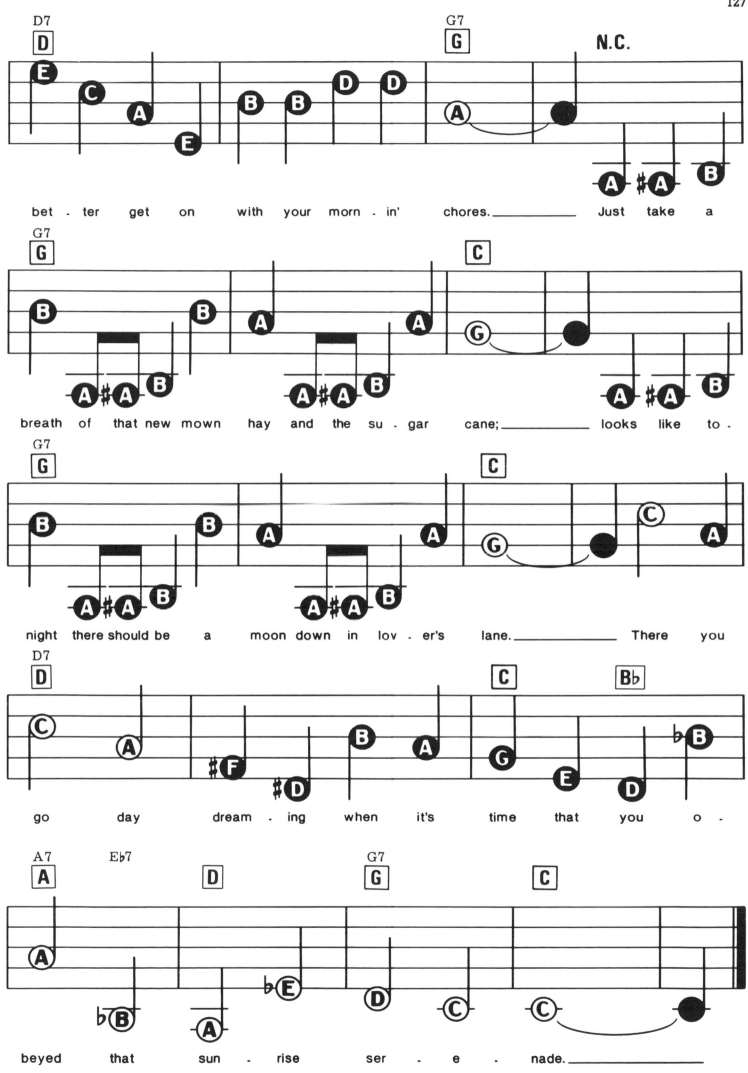

Sweet Someone

Registration 5
Rhythm: Latin or Tango

Words by George Waggner
Music by Baron Keyes

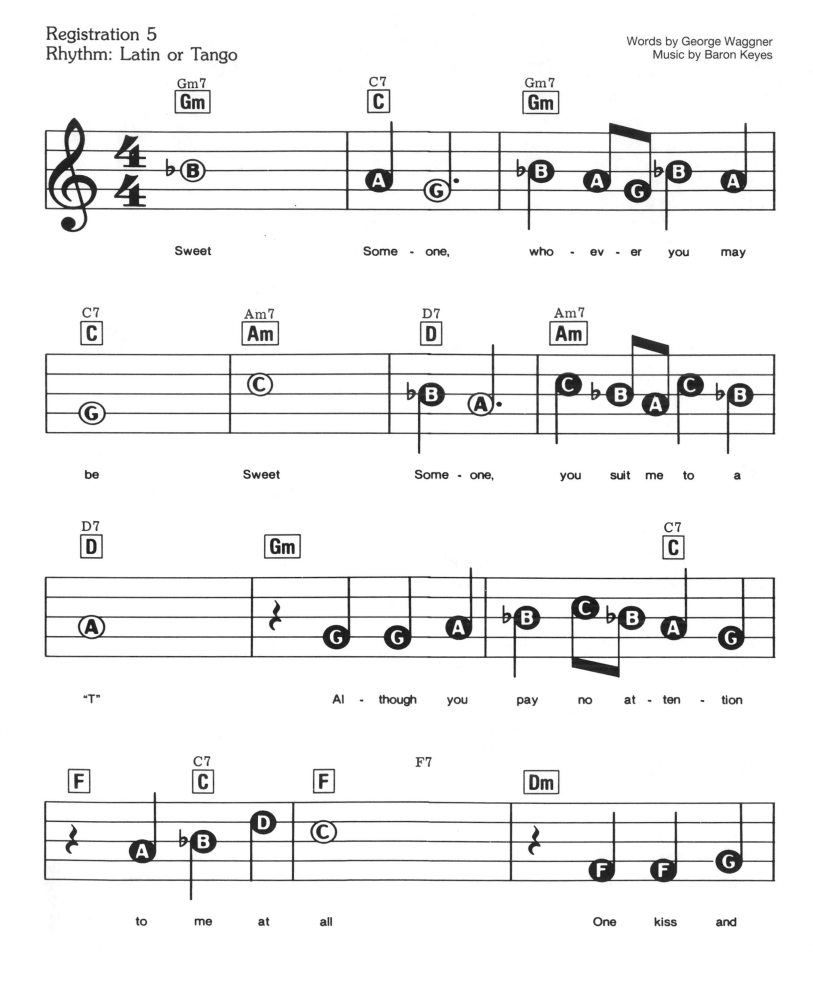

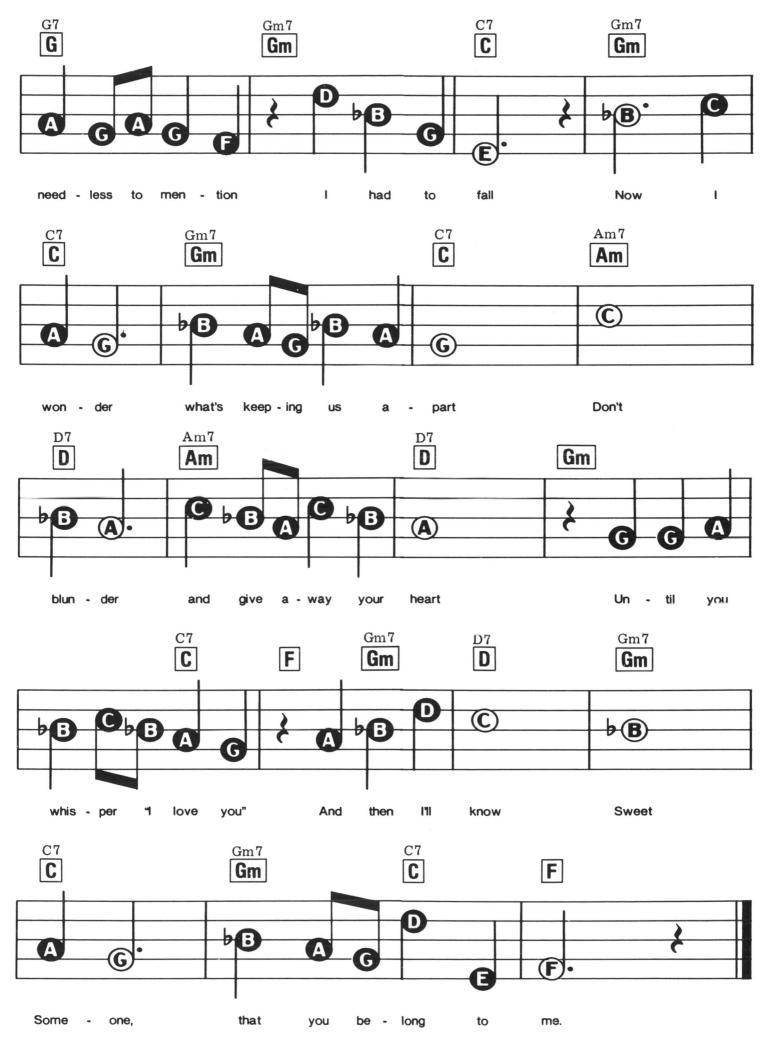

A Sunday Kind Of Love

Registration 2
Rhythm: Swing or Jazz

Words and Music by Barbara Belle, Louis Prima,
Anita Leonard and Stan Rhodes

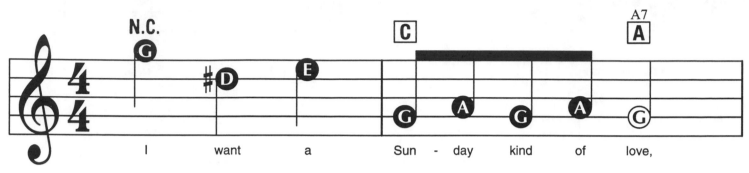

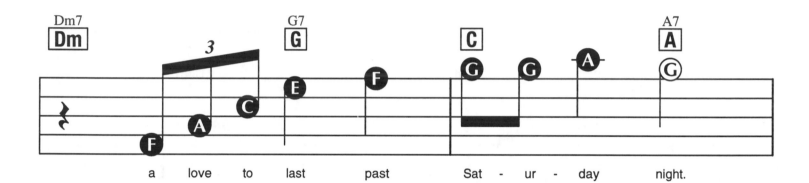

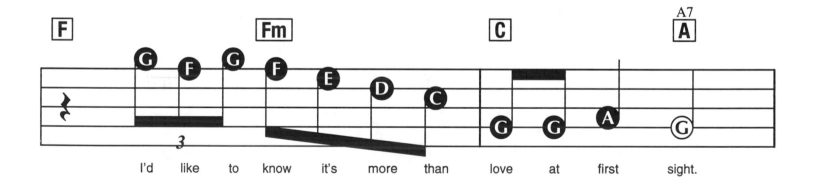

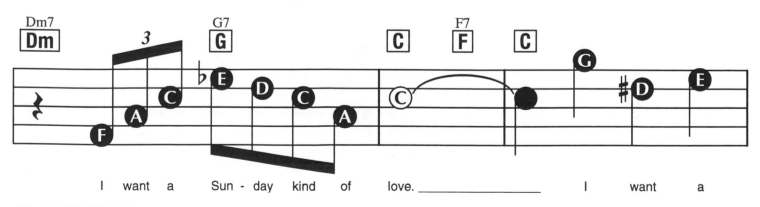

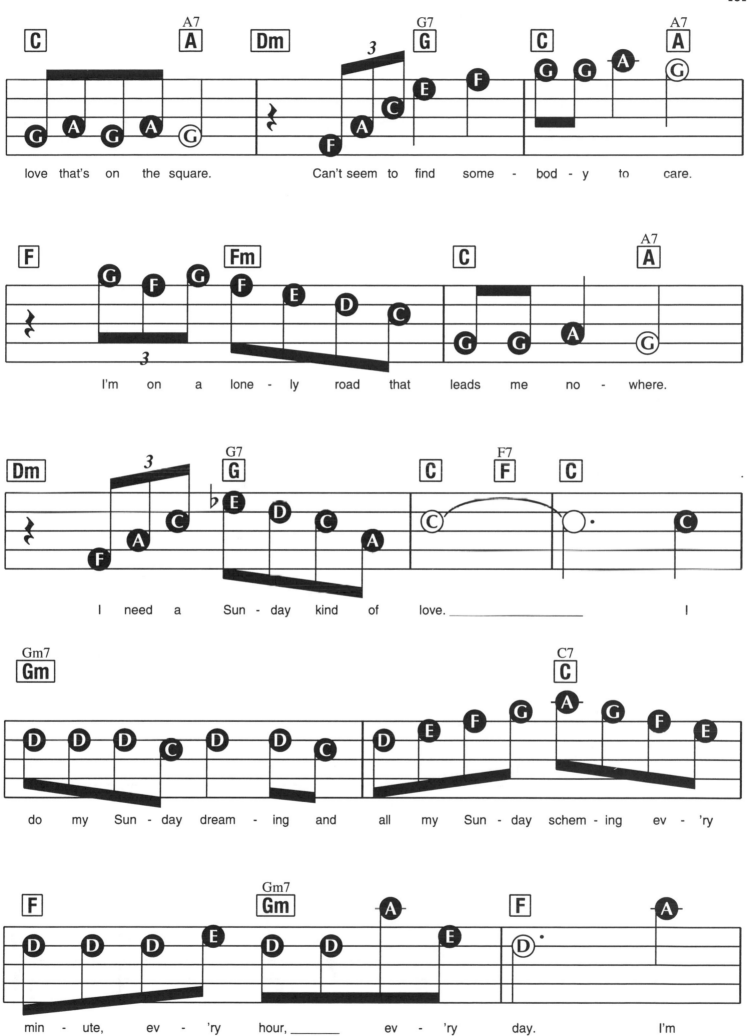

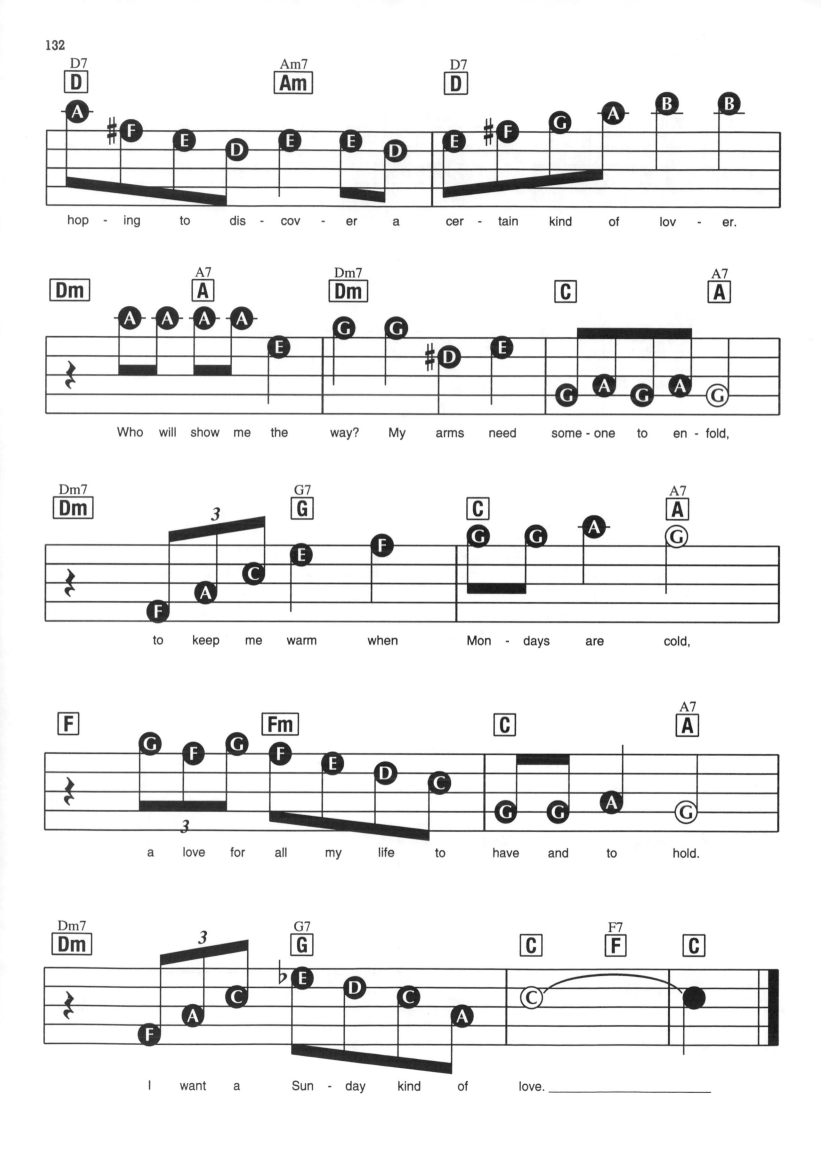

Twelfth Street Rag

Registration 5
Rhythm: Shuffle or Swing

By Euday L. Bowman

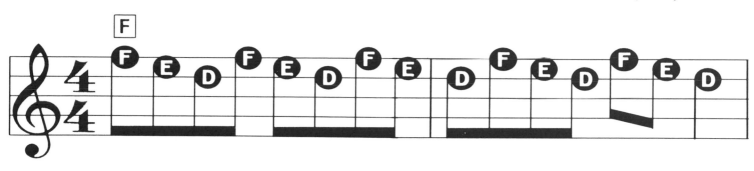

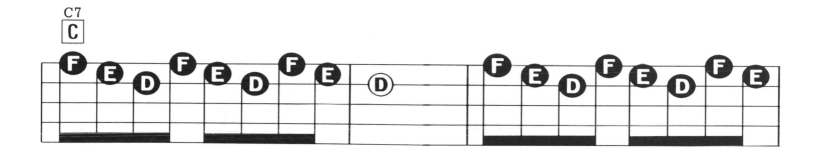

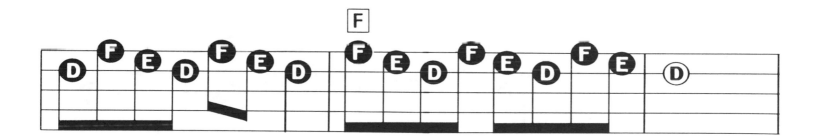

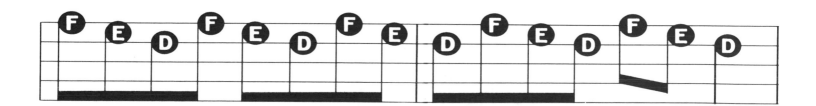

134

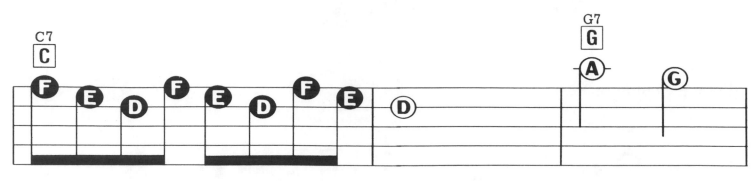

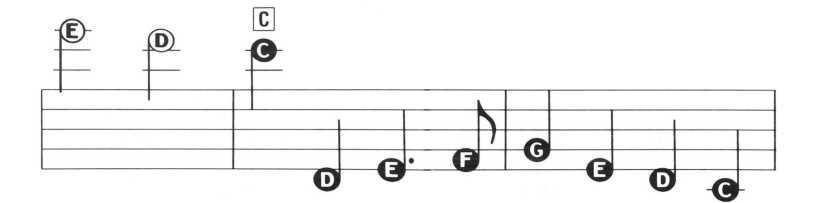

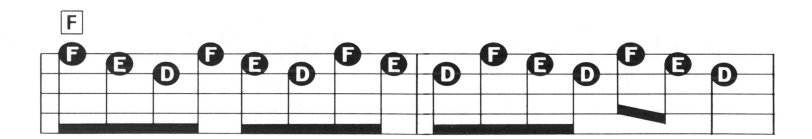

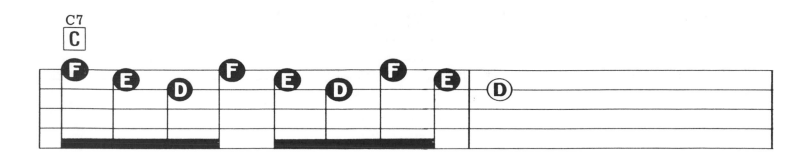

135

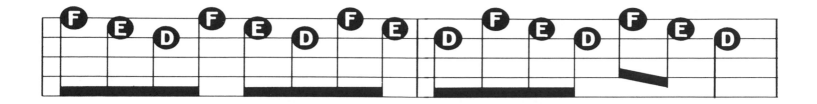

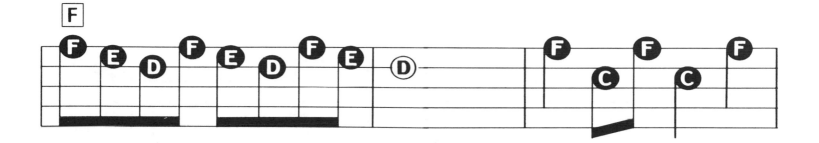

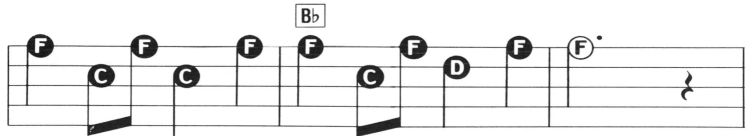

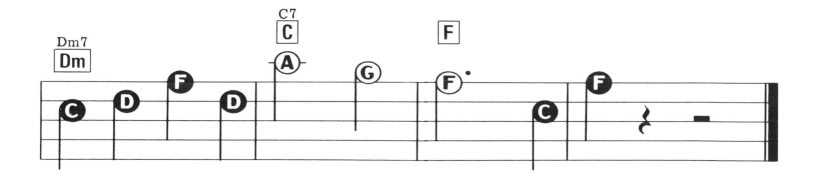

Tenderly
from TORCH SONG

Registration 2
Rhythm: Waltz

Lyric by Jack Lawrence
Music by Walter Gross

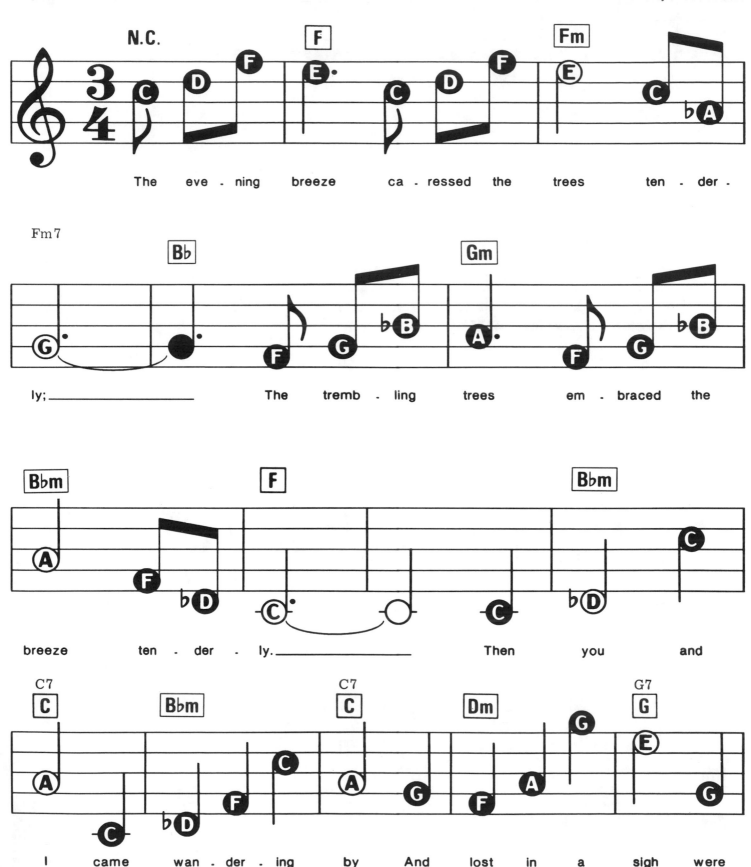

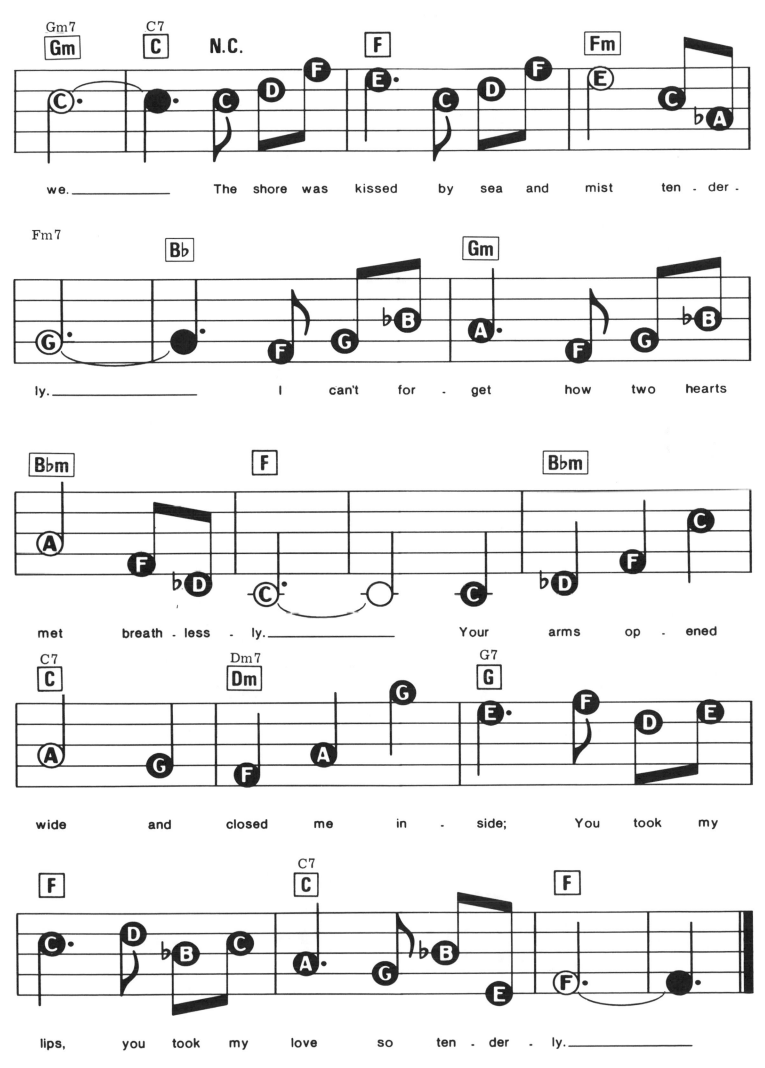

Undecided

Registration 7
Rhythm: Swing or Fox Trot

Words by Sid Robin
Music by Charles Shavers

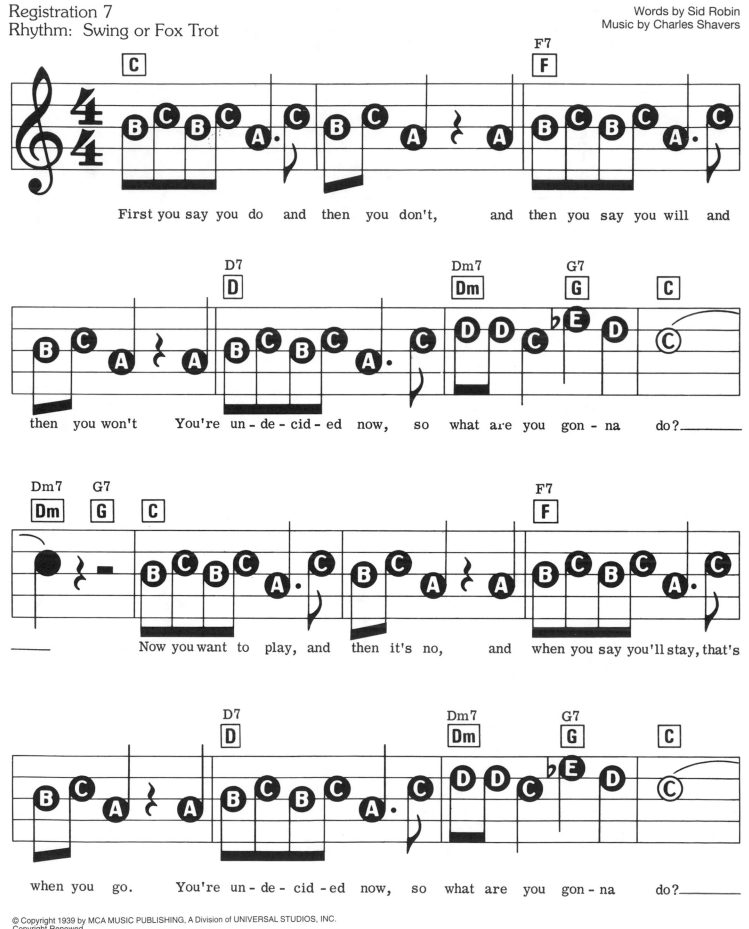

First you say you do and then you don't, and then you say you will and

then you won't You're un-de-cid-ed now, so what are you gon-na do?

Now you want to play, and then it's no, and when you say you'll stay, that's

when you go. You're un-de-cid-ed now, so what are you gon-na do?

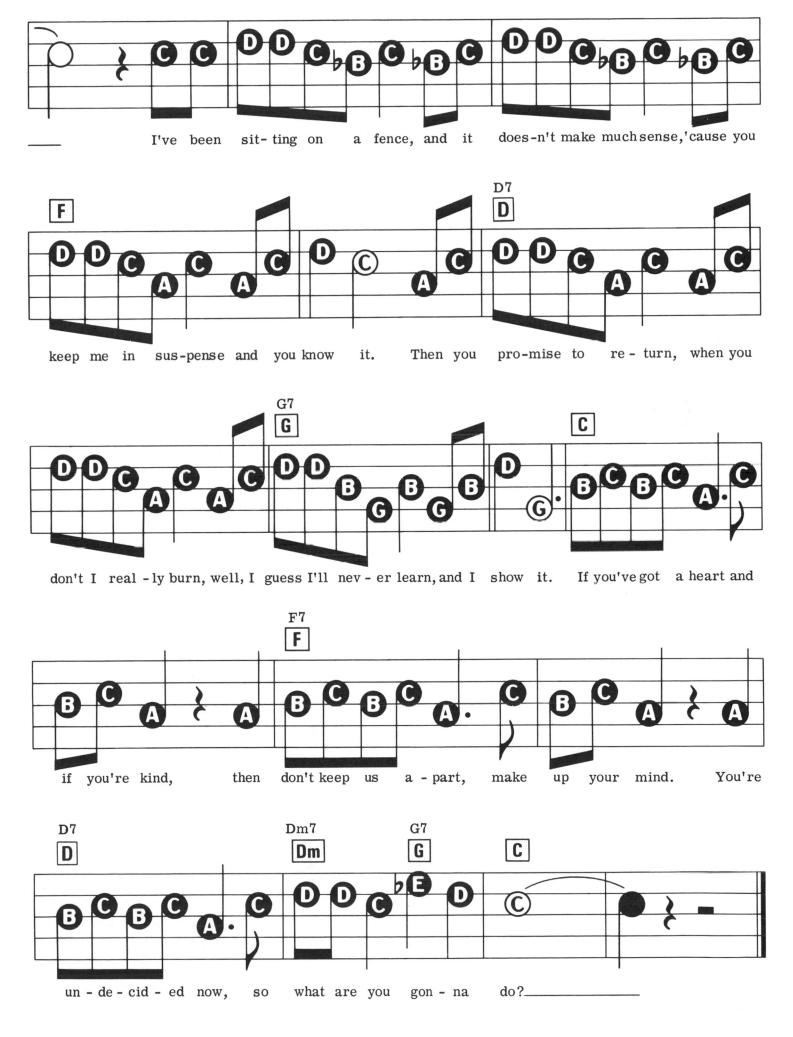

The Way You Look Tonight
from SWING TIME

Registration 3
Rhythm: Fox Trot or Swing

Words by Dorothy Fields
Music by Jerome Kern

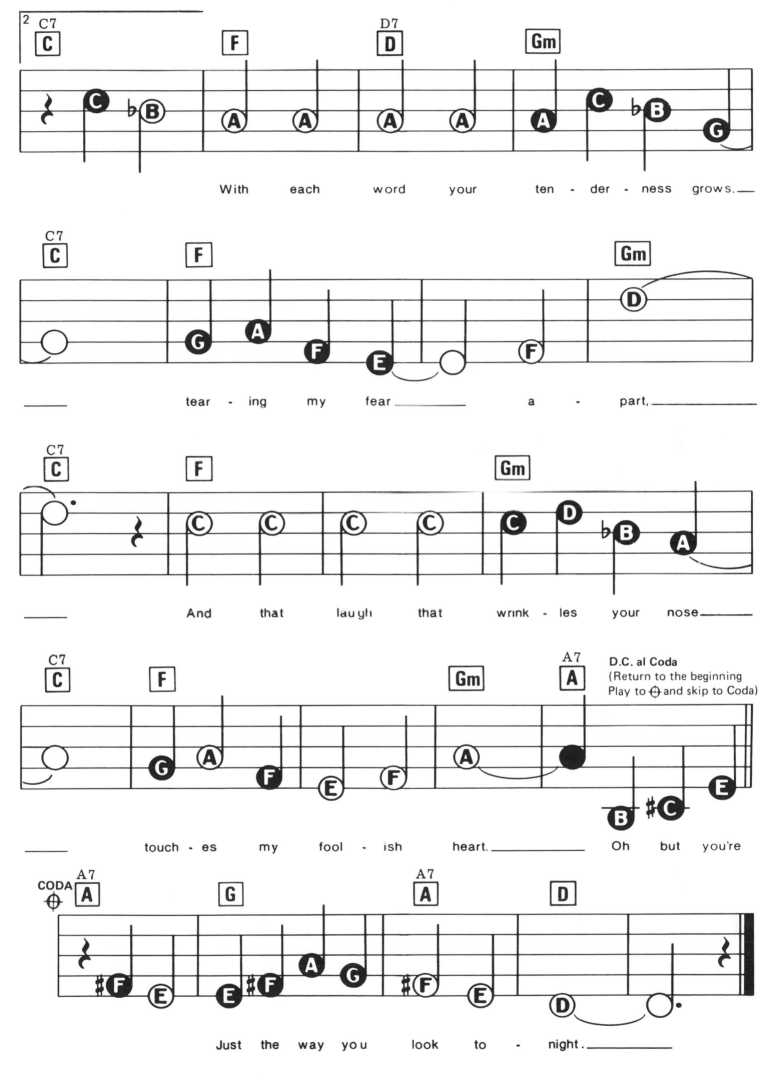

With each word your ten - der - ness grows.

tear - ing my fear a - part,

And that laugh that wrink - les your nose

touch - es my fool - ish heart. Oh but you're

Just the way you look to - night.

When My Baby Smiles At Me

Registration 1
Rhythm: Fox Trot or Swing

Words and Music by Harry Von Tilzer, Andrew B. Sterling,
Bill Munro and Ted Lewis

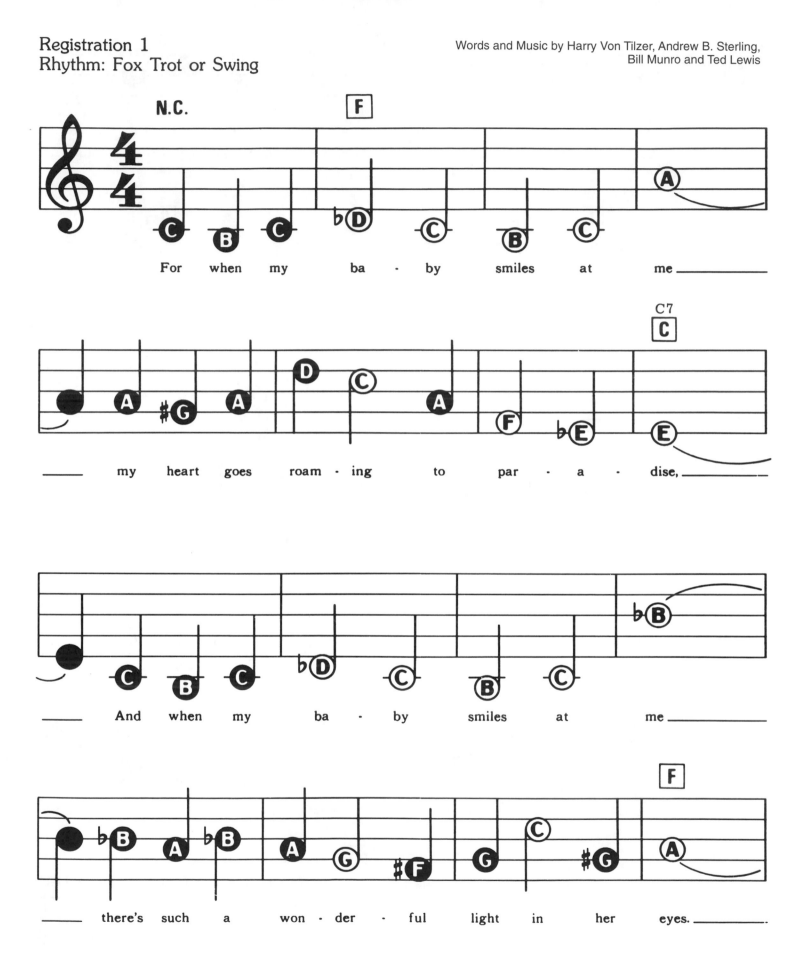

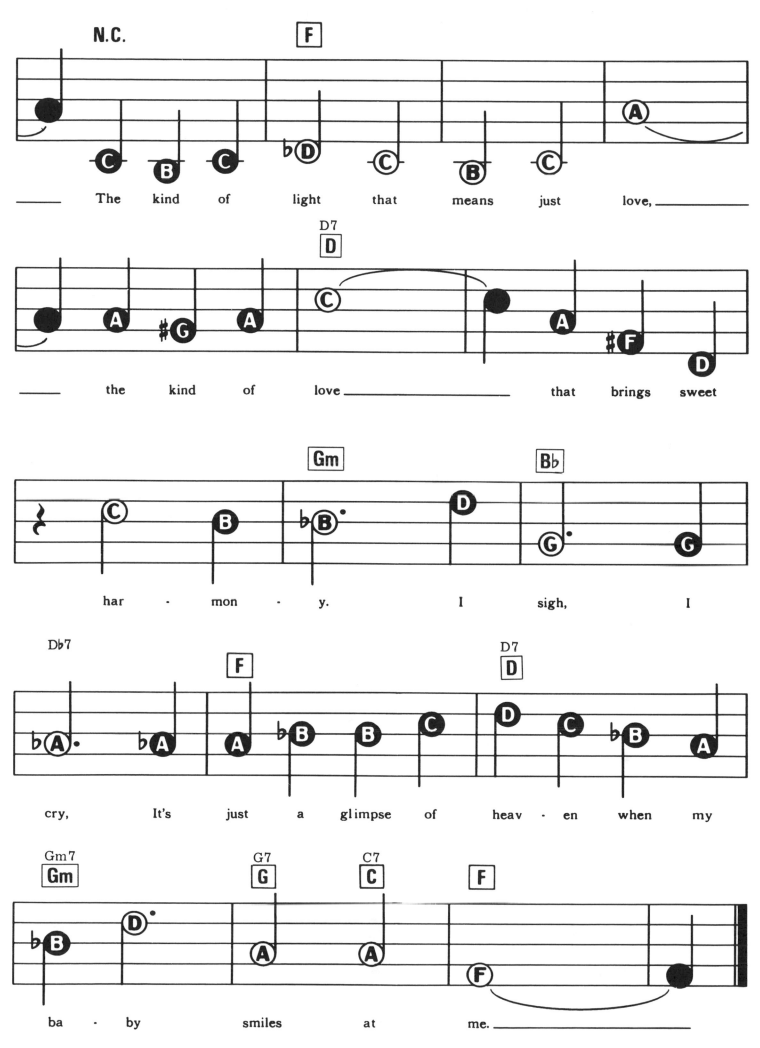

When My Sugar Walks Down The Street

Registration 5
Rhythm: Fox Trot or Swing

Words and Music by Gene Austin,
Jimmie McHugh and Irving Mills

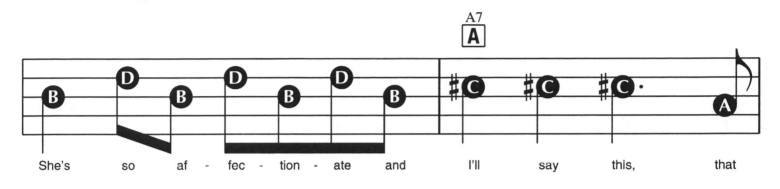

She's so af - fec - tion - ate and I'll say this, that

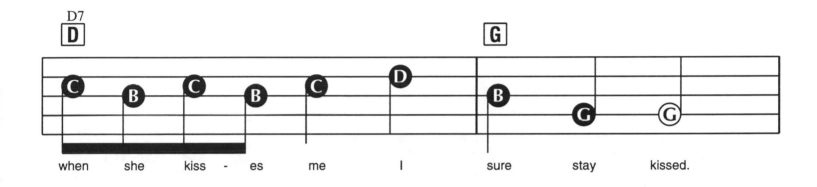

when she kiss - es me I sure stay kissed.

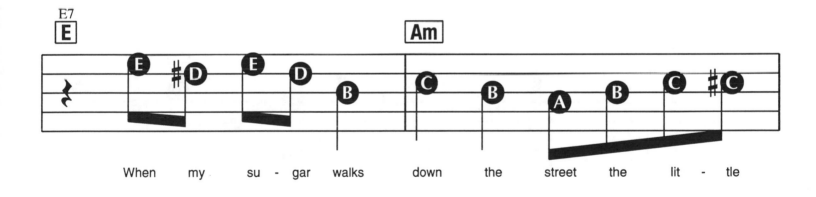

When my su - gar walks down the street the lit - tle

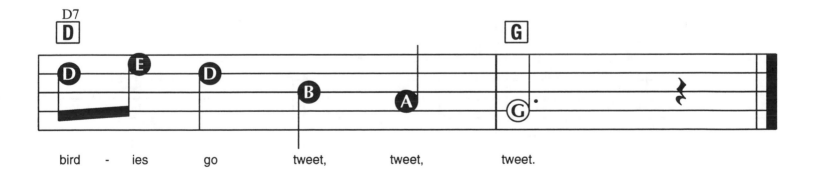

bird - ies go tweet, tweet, tweet.

When The Red, Red Robin Comes Bob, Bob, Bobbin' Along

Registration 5
Rhythm: Fox Trot or Swing

Words and Music by
Harry Woods

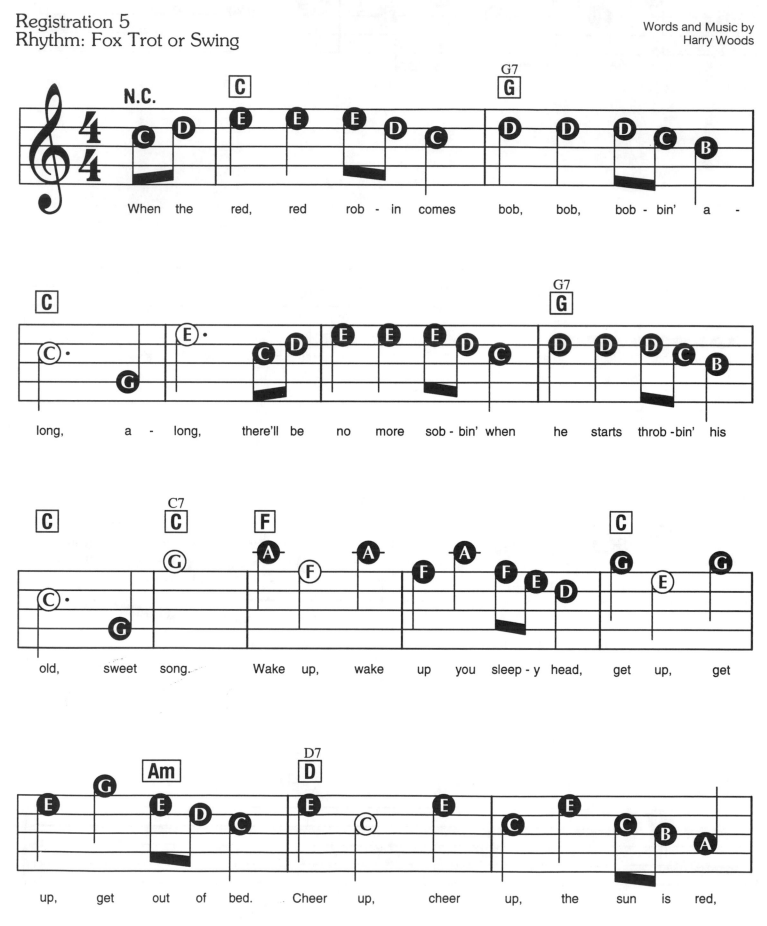

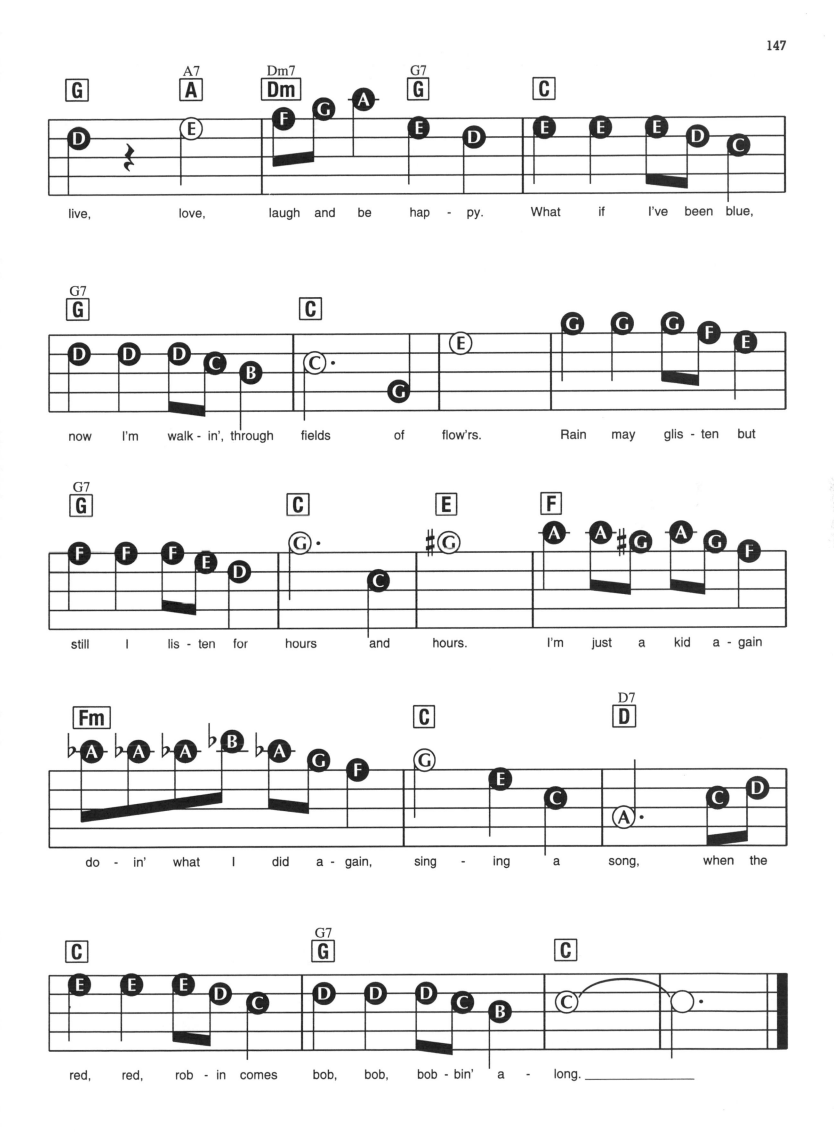

Who?
from SUNNY

Registration 1
Rhythm: Fox Trot or Swing

Lyrics by Otto Harbach and Oscar Hammerstein II
Music by Jerome Kern

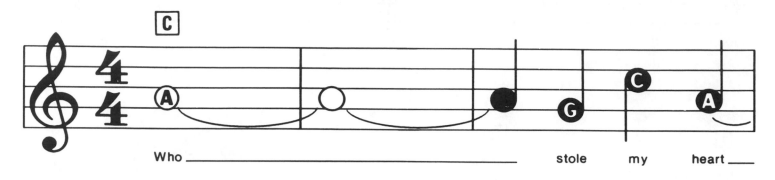

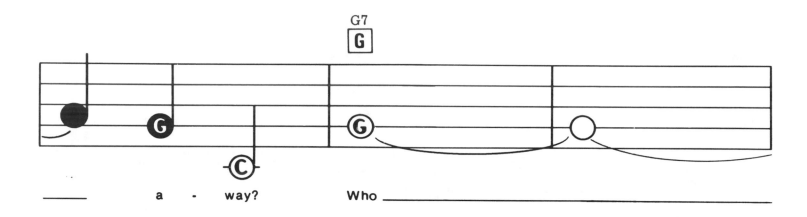

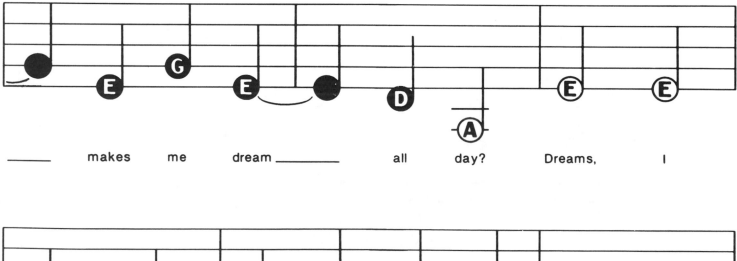

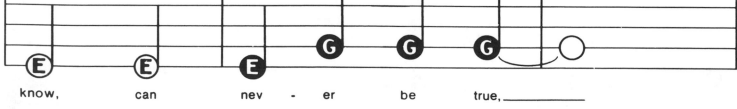

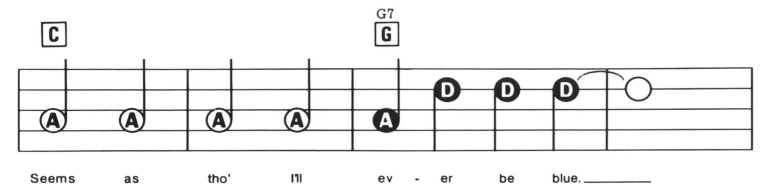

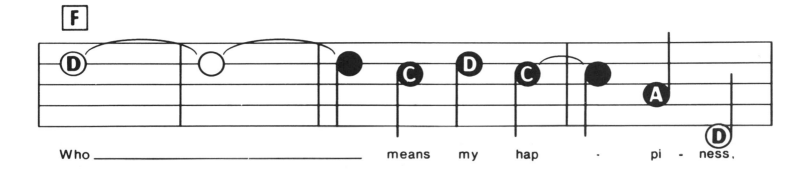

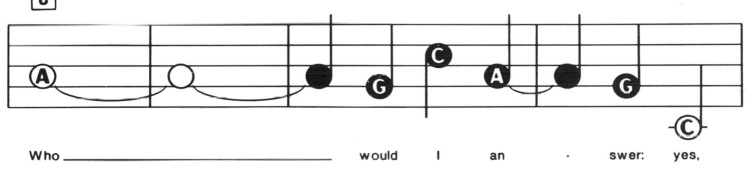

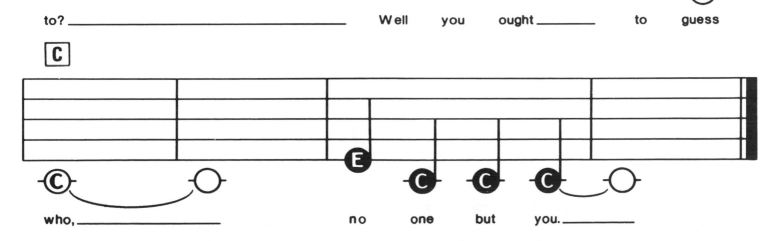

Who's Sorry Now
from THREE LITTLE WORDS

Registration 1
Rhythm: Fox Trot or Swing

Words by Bert Kalmar and Harry Ruby
Music by Ted Snyder

Who's sor - ry now?   Who's sor - ry

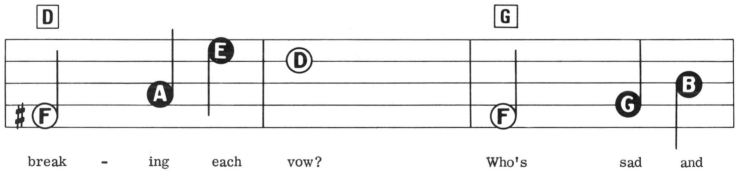

now?   Whose heart is ach - ing for

break - ing each vow?   Who's sad and

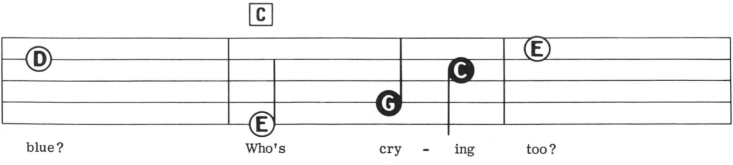

blue?   Who's cry - ing too?

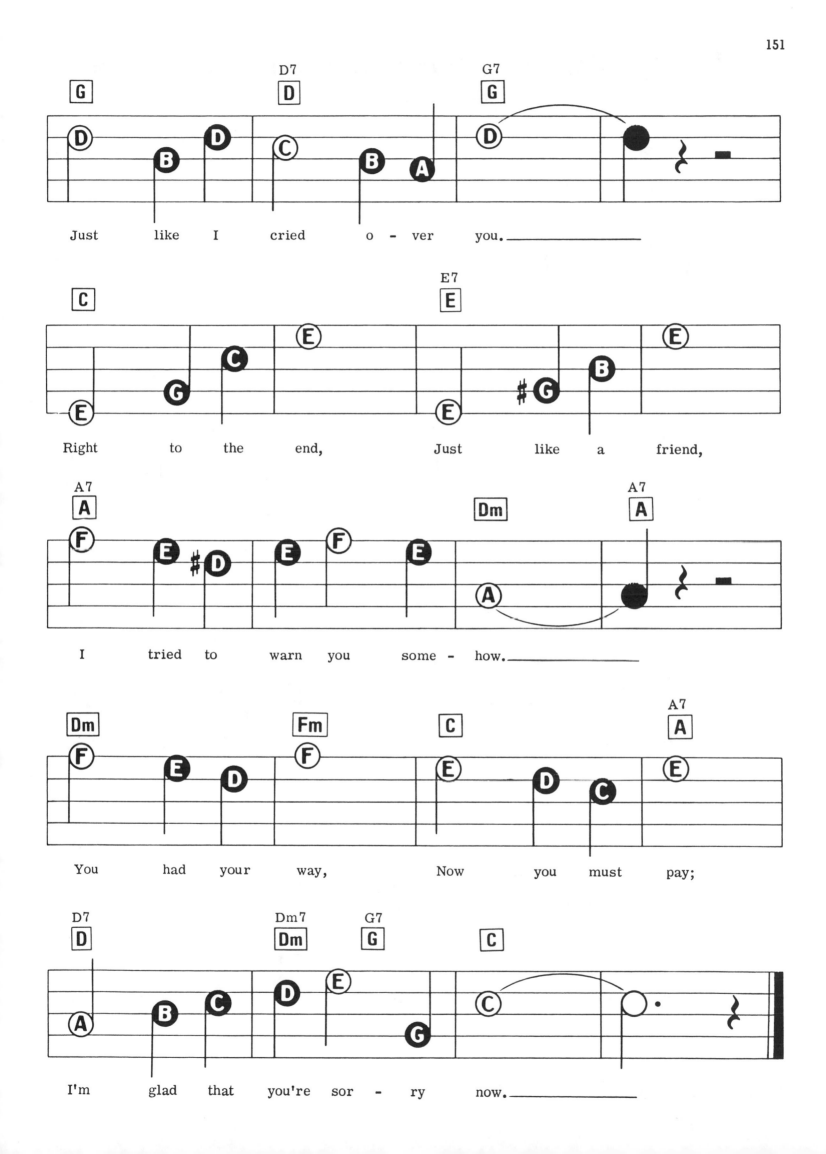

Wrap Your Troubles In Dreams
(And Dream Your Troubles Away)

Registration 4
Rhythm: Fox Trot

Lyric by Ted Koehler and Billy Moll
Music by Harry Barris

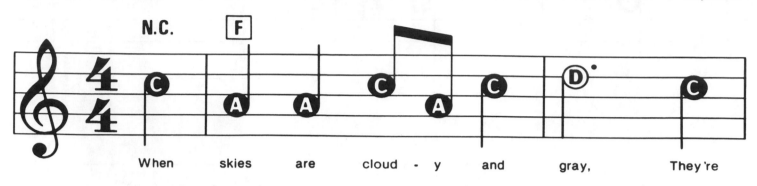

When skies are cloud - y and gray, They're

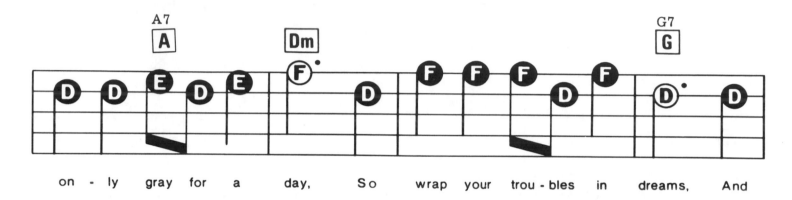

on - ly gray for a day, So wrap your trou - bles in dreams, And

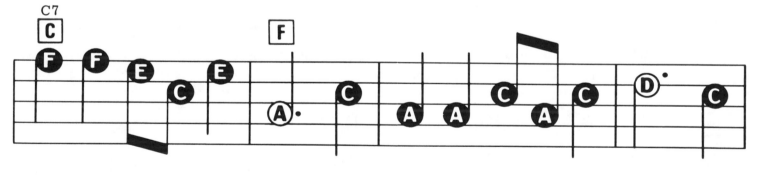

dream your trou - bles a - way, Un - til that sun - shine peeps thru, There's

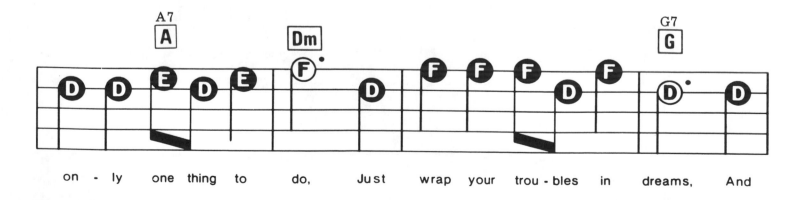

on - ly one thing to do, Just wrap your trou - bles in dreams, And

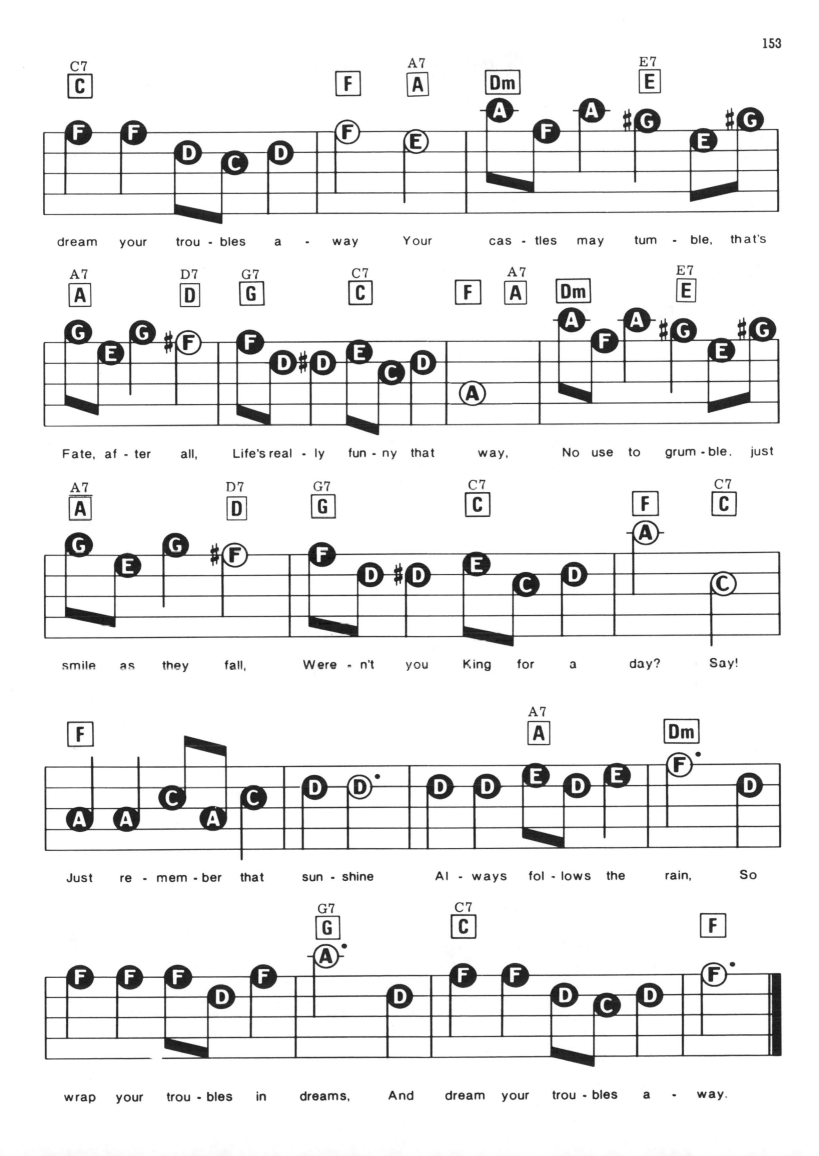

153

Yes Indeed

Registration 7
Rhythm: March

Words and Music by
Sy Oliver

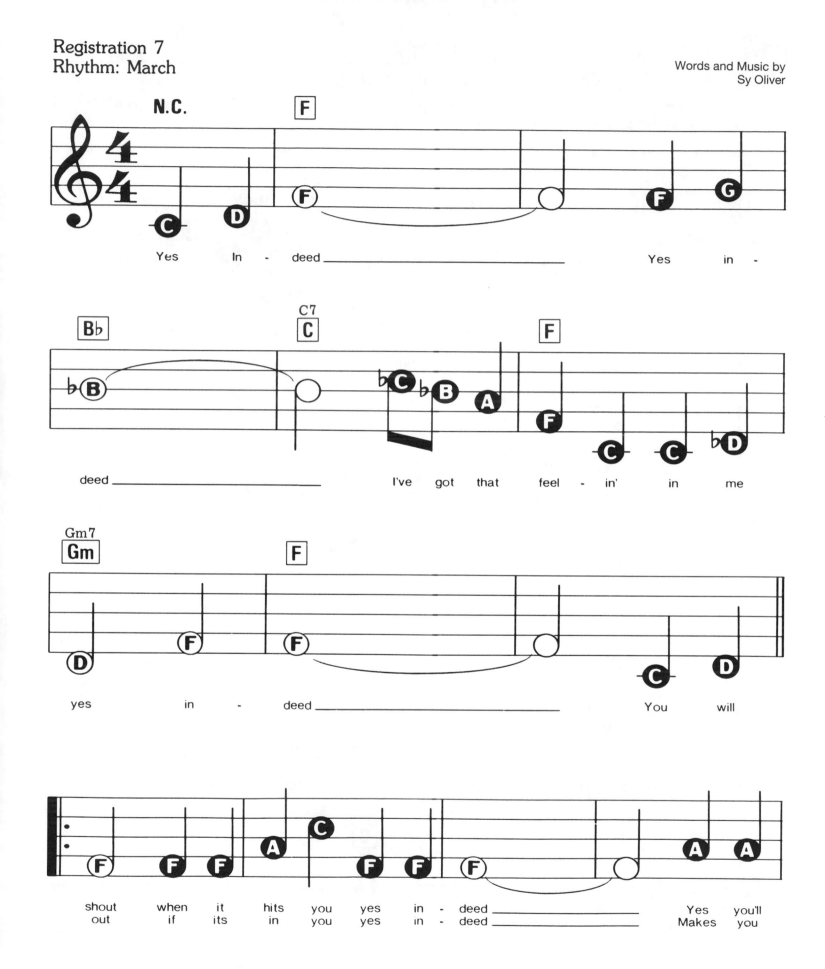

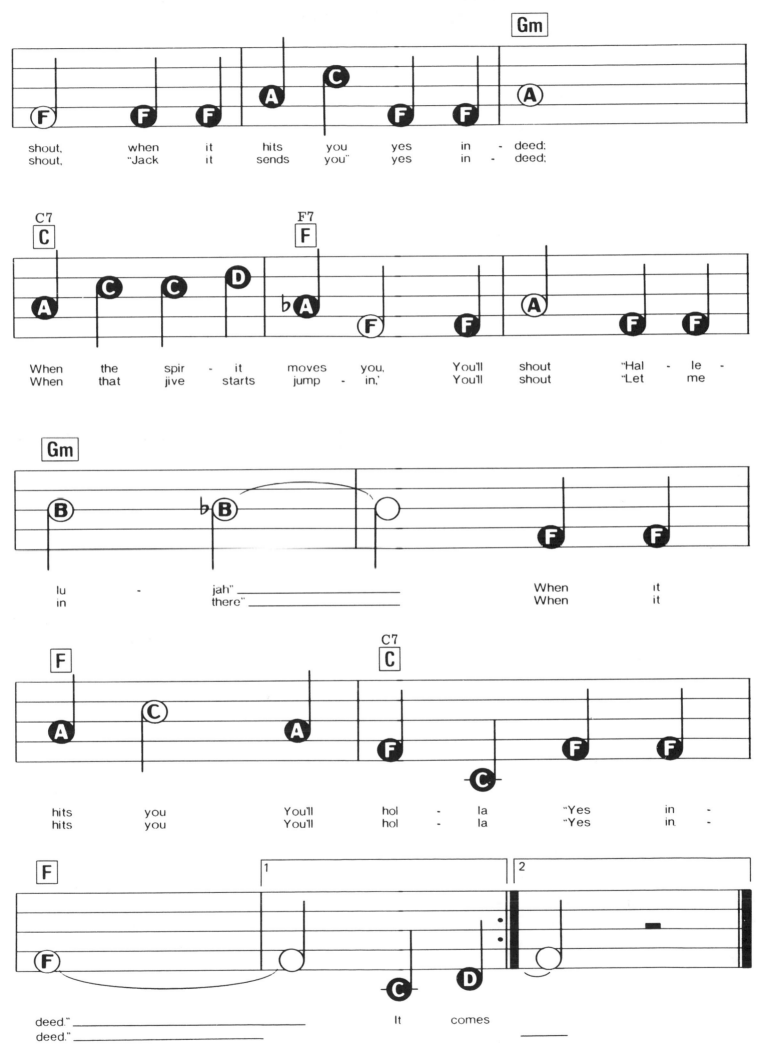

Yesterdays
from ROBERTA

Registration 10
Rhythm: Ballad or Swing

Words by Otto Harbach
Music by Jerome Kern

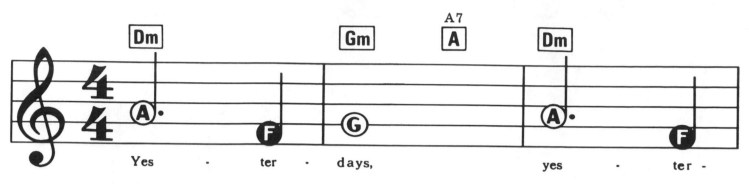

Yes - ter - days, yes - ter -

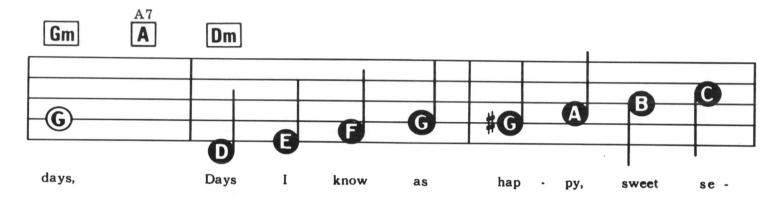

days, Days I know as hap - py, sweet se -

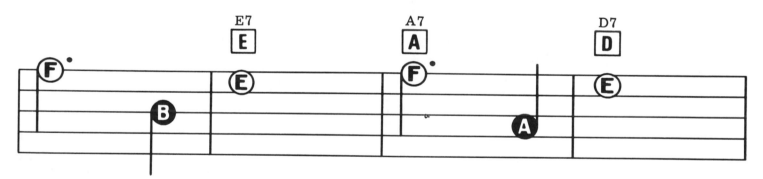

ques - ter'd days; Old - en days,

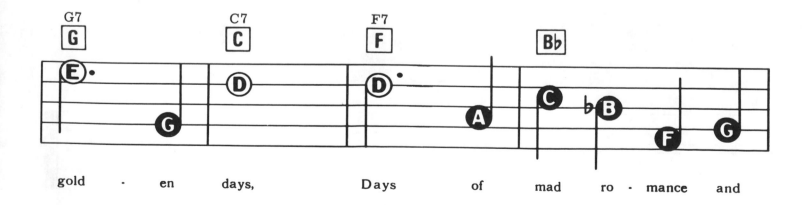

gold - en days, Days of mad ro - mance and

157

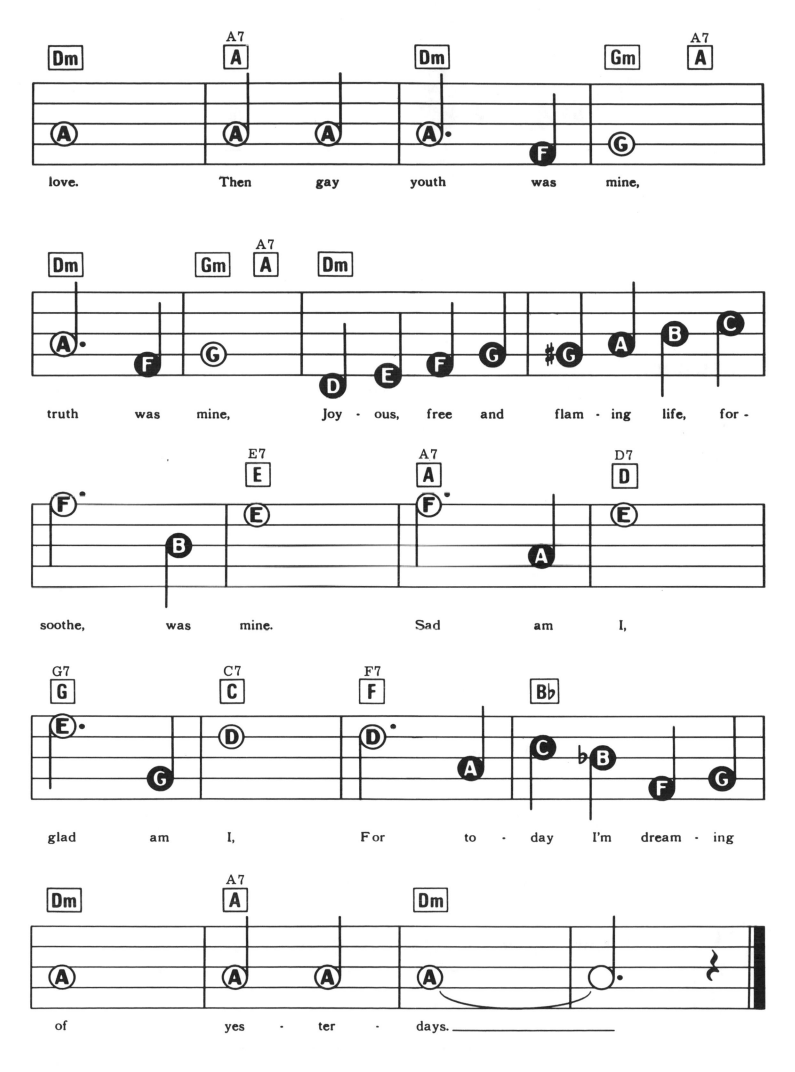

Registration Guide

- Match the Registration number on the song to the corresponding numbered category below. Select and activate an instrumental sound available on your instrument.
- Choose an automatic rhythm appropriate to the mood and style of the song. (Consult your Owner's Guide for proper operation of automatic rhythm features.)
- Adjust the tempo and volume controls to comfortable settings.

Registration

1	Flute, Pan Flute, Jazz Flute
2	Clarinet, Organ
3	Violin, Strings
4	Brass, Trumpet, Bass
5	Synth Ensemble, Accordion, Brass
6	Pipe Organ, Harpsichord
7	Jazz Organ, Vibraphone, Vibes, Electric Piano, Jazz Guitar
8	Piano, Electric Piano
9	Trumpet, Trombone, Clarinet, Saxophone, Oboe
10	Violin, Cello, Strings